P9-DFZ-999

Praise for Patrick Kavanaugh's *You Are Talented!* from a variety of talent fields

Music

"*You Are Talented!* is a helpful book in a neglected area. Dr. Kavanaugh gives specific guidelines on using one's talents for the Lord's service. Using biblical references, he shows us how to evaluate ability and use it effectively. This book opened my eyes!"

Steven E. Hendrickson, principal trumpet,
National Symphony Orchestra

Home

"In this practical and well-thought-out guide to discovering and employing our God-given talents, Dr. Patrick Kavanaugh challenges and inspires ordinary people to attempt the extraordinary for the glory of God."

Melanie M. Jeschke, home-schooling mother of nine children, pastor's wife and author of the novel Inklings
(Book 1 of The Oxford Chronicles*)*

Theater

"In our high-speed world, Doing takes precedence over Being. Kavanaugh's book reminds us that our talents are God-given and come with the invitation to stay connected to the Giver. As our minds and hearts are refreshed, our talents engage with the culture as expressions of excellence, integrity and grace."

Scott Nolte, producing artistic director,
Taproot Theatre Company

Business

"There are many books that address sharpening skills, but Dr. Kavanaugh uses a unique conversational style to address sharpening your talents and perfecting your work product for greater service to the Lord. This concept is far too often overlooked as we Christians fill our lives with activity but with little focus on results and what we can give back to God in return for the talents and opportunities He gave us. I recommend adding Dr. Kavanaugh's *You Are Talented!* to a valuable collection of leadership books."

Marc Schulman, operations executive, Fortune 100 company

Dance

"Patrick Kavanaugh has written a powerful book that not only speaks affirmation to the heart of the artist, but leaves the reader with a deep appreciation of God's workmanship in our everyday lives. You will be left with a renewed passion to explore your God-given talents."

Steve Rooks, former principal dancer,
Martha Graham Dance Company

Teaching

"The simple title of this book belies the many truths it packs and the rich ways in which those truths are presented. This is no mere self-help treatise; this is both a celebration of the limitless outpouring of talents, great and small, that our heavenly Father graciously bestows on all His children, and a compelling challenge to refine those talents and put them into excellent practice, first and foremost for His glory, as well as for the edification of others. From dishwashers to dignitaries, presidents to postmen, Pat ushers in a wide host of historical figures as examples of the challenges and glories of recognizing that no talent is too small to render as rich service to Christ, nor too weak to grow in disciplined excellence."

Hugh Sung, instructor, The Curtis Institute

Science

"In this book Dr. Kavanaugh has addressed the topic of using one's God-given talents in everyday situations. He has done so in a style that is both clear and logical. The book includes a practical guide for identifying and utilizing one's own talents. I strongly recommend it for all Christians who have ever waited for other, more talented brethren to do the job that God intended them to do."

Dr. Charles Davis, co-founder of and chief scientist for the
Department of Defense's Fiber Optic Sensor System (FOSS) program, author of From Genes to Genesis

You Are Talented!

Discovering, Perfecting and Using Your Unique Abilities

Patrick Kavanaugh

Chosen Books

A Division of Baker Book House Co
Grand Rapids, Michigan 49516

© 2002 by Patrick Kavanaugh

Published by Chosen Books
A division of Baker Book House Company
P.O. Box 6287, Grand Rapids, MI 49516-6287

Printed in the United States of America

All rights reserved. No part of this publication may be reproduced, stored in a retrieval system, or transmitted in any form or by any means—for example, electronic, photocopy, recording—without the prior written permission of the publisher. The only exception is brief quotations in printed reviews.

Library of Congress Cataloging-in-Publication Data

Kavanaugh, Patrick.
    You are talented! : discovering, perfecting, and using your unique abilities / Patrick Kavanaugh.
        p.   cm.
    ISBN 0-8007-9306-4 (pbk.)
    1. Gifts—Religious aspects—Christianity. I. Title.
BR115.G54 .K38 2002
248.4—dc21   2002005396

Unless otherwise noted, Scripture is taken from the HOLY BIBLE, NEW INTERNATIONAL VERSION®. NIV®. Copyright © 1973, 1978, 1984 by International Bible Society. Used by permission of Zondervan Publishing House. All rights reserved.

Scripture marked KJV is taken from the King James Version of the Bible.

For current information about all releases from Baker Book House, visit our web site:
                    http://www.bakerbooks.com

To my dear friends,
Nick and Donna Tavani,
and their very talented family

Contents

Foreword

I. Am. Talented. There, I said it. Have you any idea how difficult that is? How many voices I had to fight just to get those three words out? So why is this confession so tongue-bitingly difficult to say? Am I afraid you will think me vain? Am I more afraid you will disagree or perhaps even laugh? Why is it so difficult to see what God has built into our lives? What invisible barrier keeps us from moving beyond this simple problem and on into a productive and creative life? In the end, is this not more an indication of our lack of understanding of God rather than of ourselves?

If we are ever able to be finally freed up and confess that God has indeed wrapped something of value up in our lives, our questions have only begun. What are gifts and which ones might I have? Is there a difference between a gift and a talent? Once I determine what my talents are, what am I supposed to do with them? What do I do with my nervousness? Who can I look to for help and encouragement? Where can I discover, hone and use my talents? Who should become the focus of my talents? What does God have to do in all this?

With a remarkable combination of wisdom, biblical understanding and common sense, Patrick Kavanaugh will deal with all these questions and, along the way, will find even better ones to ask. This is an owner's manual for talents. From the wealth of his repertoire of experience, he will help you and me understand how to develop and improve our God-given talents. He will redefine many of our shallow definitions. The truth of most of what he says is self-evident. The rest you will have to trust him for until you realize the truth of it in your own creative experience. He will show us how to invite God into this process. He will help us see how, in fact, He has been at the heart of the process all along; how He *is* the heart of it. Patrick will counsel us to be patient with the process. His is a voice that inspires patience.

Having said all this, I now hand you off to my friend Patrick. Walk with him through these pages and listen. You will find that you will learn to see and seek to further understand the amazing work God has created in you—what gifts and talents He has wrapped up in your life. To see and then to turn and offer them back in worshipful obedience.

Michael Card

Introduction

"To one he gave five talents of money, to another two talents, and to another one talent, each according to his ability."

Matthew 25:15

Talent. What scenes does this word suggest to your imagination? Are they scenes of competition; of winners (and losers) in talent shows; of split-second Olympic time trials and musical superstars; of quarterbacks and homecoming queens; of tension-filled contests in which second place counts for nothing?

Or do you imagine a grandfather telling stories to a group of spellbound children; a middle-aged woman working late in a flower garden; a schoolboy finding a clever way to include a new classmate in the games at recess; a mother triumphantly setting a delicious meal before her hungry family; a mason grateful to spend his life perfecting an obscure corner of a cathedral; or a young musician practicing an extra hour to improve a few difficult passages?

The world tries to convince us that there are two types of people: the talented and the untalented. The Bible shows this perspective to be false. God created every one of us with specific inborn talents. Some have this one, some have that one, and each of us has differing degrees of various talents. But we are all talented, and it has nothing to do with whether we "deserve" our talents or not. God "sends rain on the righteous and the unrighteous" (Matthew 5:45).

Every talent you have ever seen on display has its origin in God. He is the great Giver of all gifts. The Scriptures make this abundantly clear: "Every good and perfect gift is from above, coming down from the Father of the heavenly lights, who does not change like shifting shadows" (James 1:17). The talents He continues to pour out on all of us are beyond measure, enabling His creatures to manifest great accomplishment, and resulting in every invention and advancement of the centuries. All this comes from the Lord! As the poet Elizabeth Barrett Browning reminds us, "God's gifts put man's best dreams to shame."

Yet many of us believe we are untalented—without gifts, appreciation or worth. The reasons we sometimes feel this way can be grouped into two broad categories:

1. We have often not fully discovered, appreciated or honed the talents God has given us.
2. The talents we have been given are not those that are typically recognized and applauded as talents (as the popular artistic or athletic talents are).

Whatever giftings we have been given, God wants to help us discover and use them for His work. In the same way that "to search out a matter is the glory of kings," (Proverbs 25:2), so we must search out our talents. Indeed, they are indispensable to God's call on our lives, an integral part of our purpose in this world.

Often when Christians do not know what it is that God wants them to do with their lives, they are unsure of the gifts that are still lying dormant within them. For if the Lord has a certain task for you to accomplish, then He will have made sure you have all the necessary equipment for the mission. The trustworthy soldier is keenly aware of each piece of his equipment and practices to have a thorough knowledge of the use of every item. In the same way, if we are to live a victorious Christian life, we must *discover*, *perfect* and *use* our talents. It is for this purpose that this book was written.

Those three words—*discover*, *perfect* and *use*—divide the book into three parts of three chapters each. The first part has to do with discovering and identifying our inborn talents—a lifetime process of stewardship that is portrayed throughout the Bible. In the second part we learn how to maximize our talents through training, discipline and long-term preparation. The third part gives practical applications of using our talents for the Lord—at home, at church and in the workplace.

As executive director of the Christian Performing Artists' Fellowship, I have spent many years working with talented believers who are actively using their skills for the Lord. I have been privileged to see the fruit of thousands of hours of diligence come forth in inspiring concerts by world-class performers. It is deeply gratifying to observe someone who has discovered his or her God-given talents, worked years to perfect them, and is now reaping the wonderful rewards of this discipline and labor.

But not all my life is spent with the superstars of today's performing arts world. I have also been a minister of music at a local church, where I have contact with dozens of talented Christians. I have worked with the boy who wants to learn a few chords on the guitar, with the flute player who will never make it to Carnegie Hall but who still desires to use her talents to worship God, and with the many sopranos who cannot sing at the Metropolitan Opera yet can be vessels of the Lord in their local church.

It is a unique opportunity, working regularly with people who come from vastly different places on the "talent scale," from world-famous performers to unknown teenagers. The diversity ever before me has prompted many questions and issues:

> Why does God sometimes give great talents to very undeserving people and seemingly withhold them from very deserving people?

> What does one do with the frustration that results from not being as talented in a certain area as you would really like to be?

> What about the person who has a tremendous amount of talent, but whose difficult circumstances keep it from being utilized?

> Why is it that some people who may be very talented receive much less reward from the world than others who may be only moderately talented?

> Why does God often seem to put us in situations in which we have little natural talent and keep us away from situations in which our true talents could really shine?

It is for questions such as these, and a thousand others, that this book is written. It is offered to all the millions who have struggled with such enigmatic questions and yet have made the undaunted commitment to use their talents for Christ.

Part 1

Discovering Your Talents

one

The Talented Christian

Each man has his own gift from God; one has this gift, another has that.

                                        1 Corinthians 7:7

What would you call a man in his fifties who, despite many patient attempts at training, could not master the most basic arithmetic? Mathematically deficient? Intellectually challenged? An idiot?

Or should you call him a genius, one of the most talented humans ever to walk on the earth?

You decide. For in this case I am referring to Ludwig van Beethoven, considered by many to be the greatest composer of all time. Even while he was writing his sublime Symphony No. 9, his young nephew was trying daily—without success—to teach his Uncle Ludwig basic arithmetic.

How can this be? How can someone compose such complex masterpieces as the Beethoven symphonies and yet be at such a complete loss in simple mathematics? The answer lies in the above Scripture from 1 Corinthians. It is true that God gives everyone gifts. It is not true that God gives everyone *every* gift.

Beethoven was given tremendous talent in music. Yet he was not given much in the way of arithmetic skills. It was as if that specific chip was left out of his computer when he was being assembled. Indeed, many other chips were also left out. He was, for instance, exceedingly slovenly. The master once dryly commented about himself, "Beethoven can compose, thank God, but he can do nothing else."

The Rarity of a "Renaissance Man"

Beethoven's case is not as unique as you may think. In all of history, it is rare to find a true "Renaissance man." That is, God seldom creates a man or woman like Michelangelo or Leonardo da Vinci—one who seems to possess a great quantity of *different* talents. And even in these unique cases, some talents are lacking.

Recently I toured the home near Oxford of the renowned twentieth-century apologist C. S. Lewis. Noticing an old typewriter, I asked the guide if this was the typewriter Lewis used to write his many great books. The guide smiled and said no. She then explained that Lewis wrote all of his books by hand. In fact, this literary genius was so utterly nonmechanical that he never could figure out how to use a typewriter or almost any other mechanical device.

Some time ago one of the world's greatest violinists performed at our MasterWorks Festival. This woman is an amazing musician, has many best-selling recordings and gives more than a hundred performances each year to sold-out concert halls. Yet when I asked her to say a few words at the microphone, she looked terrified. Although she is open and friendly and has a warm personality, the prospect of even a moment of public speaking was impossible.

I could tell anecdote after anecdote, but you get the idea. Many famous and talented people can hardly change a lightbulb. Some soldiers who have shown superhuman courage in battle blanch at the thought of standing in front of a church congregation. Some athletes say they cannot draw a straight line with a ruler. This is not a new revelation. The ancient Greek playwright Euripides pointed out: "The same man cannot be skilled in everything; each has his special excellence."

The Lord: A Sower of Good Seed

As we watch the superstars of this world, we often come away with the impression that "some people have *all* the talent." A closer look always shows this to be an illusion; even the most gifted are lacking in many other areas. One thinks of the "absentminded professor" type who can revel in quantum physics and yet cannot use a can opener.

This is an important point. As we examine the way in which God distributes gifts, we must first abandon a great myth about this subject: the idea that the Lord is haphazard in His talent giving, that He gives talents to a select few but not to the majority of us. Nothing could be further from the truth.

It seems this way to us because all we can see is the "visible fruit" from His talent giving. That is, we see certain people who have been diligent in discovering, perfecting and using their gifts in such a way that makes them successful. We do *not* see the millions of people who have also been given talent by God yet have not been able to discover, perfect and use their gifts—and therefore seem "untalented" to us and even to themselves.

Consider the Parable of the Sower (see Matthew 13:1–23; Mark 4:1–20; Luke 8:4–15). Jesus told this story in reference to sowing the Word—the Gospel message—but it illustrates quite well the manner in which the Lord has sown talents throughout the world. As you will recall, the sower spreads seed on four different types of soil, but only one of the four brings forth a crop. Therefore, if a passerby looks on this scene at harvesttime and sees the crop growing on the good soil, he might assume that only this land was seeded.

In the same way, we see the outward fruit only of the people who have somehow found a way to use their God-given talents successfully. We assume wrongly that these are the chosen ones, the "talented," and that the "fields" belonging to the rest of us were never sown. Like the passerby who sees the crop growing in certain soil—but who never saw the initial, even distribution of seeds—we conclude that God is a rather arbitrary giver of gifts.

Yet the good seed of God's gifts is sown deeply in every new child who is born. The problem is not that talent is lacking but that it is often not discovered and utilized. Sir Robert Walpole, who became Britain's first prime minister, remarked, "Men are often capable of greater things than they perform. They are sent into the world with bills of credit, and seldom draw to their full extent."

"Untalented" No More

We are *all* talented. Paul says, "Each man has his own gift from God" (1 Corinthians 7:7). Is Paul telling the truth? Is he exaggerating for dramatic effect? I believe that he is simply stating a fact.

Of course, some may object to applying this Scripture to talents. They state, correctly, that in this sentence Paul is referring to "spiritual gifts." (The differences between spiritual gifts and talents will be examined in a later chapter.) Nevertheless, Paul is illustrating a scriptural principle in this passage that concerns the nature of God and the manner in which He distributes gifts— that God gives them to each of His children.

My wife, who teaches private cello lessons, will occasionally talk to me about a certain new student who is not doing very well. "That poor child," she will say in frustration, "has no talent whatsoever!" But of course, what she really means is that the student does not seem to have any talent for the cello. She will (soon, let's hope) direct him to other areas of pursuit. This student may become the next Albert Einstein, Jane Austen, Billy Graham—whomever you want to name as an example of someone who has discovered, perfected and used his talent successfully.

A key Scripture on this subject is actually called the Parable of the Talents (see Matthew 25:14–30). Luke 19:11–27 records a similar story, which is usually referred to as the Parable of the Minas. The main difference between these parables has to do with the form of money given by the master to his servants: a talent or a mina. Authorities are uncertain as to their exact worth, but all agree that the servants were entrusted with financial resources.

While we recognize at the outset that the talents in this parable refer to currency, I do not believe that we are being at all unfaithful to the heart of Jesus' message if we apply its principles to physical and mental—as well as monetary—endowments.

As with all of Jesus' parables, many excellent principles can be gleaned from these two; we will, in fact,
encounter a plethora of important principles from these
two parables many times in this book. We have already
begun highlighting one of them, one that might be called
the *universality* of God's gift giving. That is, God gives
gifts to everyone; not the same gifts and not the same
amount of any one gift, but everyone receives something. Note that in both the parables of the talents and
the minas every servant is given *something* by the master. Some this amount and some that amount—but no
one is left out. Jesus does not say, "He gave to one servant zero talents." It is not in God's nature to do so.

We will see further that the number of gifts given is not
as important as what we do with the gifts we have. But
of this we can be sure: We all have been given talents. As
first-century Roman philosopher Seneca observed, "God
has given gifts to the whole human race, from which no
one is excluded."

Factors That Discourage the Development of Talent

Why then do we not see everyone, including ourselves,
successfully using his talents? This question has as many
answers as there are people. As we saw in the parable
about the sower, there are multiple reasons why three
out of four "soils" failed to produce a crop.

One factor might be the environment. That is, a child
might be born with an extraordinary talent, but her environment fails to bring it forth. Perhaps her parents are
struggling financially and cannot afford proper training. Perhaps the parents are hostile to the specific talent and actively discourage it. Or perhaps there are no
parents nearby and no one else to encourage the child's
natural gifts. All too often a child's great talent is never

discovered by his parents—or even in the person's entire lifetime. This possibility ought to admonish all parents to attempt persistently to uncover and cultivate the talents of their children.

Inborn talent is like a delicate plant. Even the finest quality seed needs positive factors in order to grow and bear fruit. There must be enough (but not too much) water and sunshine. The soil must be rich and well tended. Rocks, weeds, thorns and other hindrances must be removed. For every plant that fully develops, many others do not. In the same way, even the finest inborn talent can wither and die without the proper care.

If a child is given tremendous artistic talent but is born into a poor farming family that needs his physical labors, will it ever be discovered? Perhaps, but perhaps not. Suppose Beethoven had never been exposed to music. (Doubtless this has happened to millions of would-be musicians throughout history.) He certainly would not have gone far as a mathematician!

Indeed, for many centuries it was customary for children to have very limited opportunities to display their inborn gifting. If a son's father was a carpenter, then it was understood that he, too, would become a carpenter. If the father was a miller, the son was to become a miller—even if he had the talent to be a writer. The options for daughters were even more limited. Praise God that, at least for most of us, we have today the personal freedom to explore and perfect our God-given talents and to choose careers and avocations accordingly!

A second factor that affects development of our talents is our health, or the lack thereof. A sickly child will have a difficult time becoming an athlete. The genius of a great violinist can be quickly silenced if she suffers hearing loss.

Yet there are inspiring exceptions to the rule. Their stories are legendary: the top track star who as a child suffered severe leg burns, the great writer who was born deaf and dumb, the thousands of talented people who have overcome bitter poverty and insurmountable obstacles to reach great goals. These stories admonish us not to blame our failings on our backgrounds or upbringing. As the angel Gabriel assured Mary, "Nothing is impossible with God" (Luke 1:37).

On our property stands a tall oak tree tightly surrounded by three large rocks. When you examine them closely, you can see that the three rocks could fit together perfectly if the tree were lifted out. They were, in fact, once all part of a huge boulder. The growing oak actually split the boulder and pushed its way through the solid rock as it grew! The picture of a little acorn lying under a boulder is a rather discouraging one. (Ever feel this way?) To see this oak reaching for the sky, having overcome such an obstacle, is truly inspiring.

A third factor that discourages the development of talent is the misapplication of one's genetic profile.

The theory exists that everything within you at your birth, including your talents, is a result of all that was within your parents, grandparents and so on. Someone might conclude, for example, that he could not have any talent for training horses because most of his family members are afraid of animals. Such an exclusive belief in genetics is erroneous. You might have talents that have no bearing on your ancestors' interests.

By the same token, we need to be sure not to go too far in the other direction and discard the idea that we inherit any traits from our families. Your genetic profile plays a large part in determining your life. It is important to examine your family's talents to help discover your own.

My wife and I are professional musicians. It is therefore not surprising to find that several of our children (not all) have demonstrated musical talent. Nevertheless, neither my parents nor, to my knowledge, any of my relatives has the slightest interest in music. How do we account for this?

Let's take a few other cases. In one of my previous books I listed many great composers who came from musical families. The list included Bach, Mozart, Beethoven and Stravinsky. Then I listed many other masters who came from families where no musical talent had ever been manifested, such as Mendelssohn, Paganini, Franck and Verdi. It is interesting to note that the two lists are about equal in size.

While my expertise is in music, I suspect that the information in the above paragraph is similarly borne out in other areas of talent. As I have a passion for reading biography and history, I have examined the lives of many renowned writers, military and political leaders, artists and inventors. Many came from families where their gifts were obviously inherited, such as General Robert E. Lee, whose father was also an adroit general. But just as many individuals who were outstanding in their fields seemed to spring up from the most unpromising family stock.

It is not unusual to find great differences even among siblings. I mentioned C. S. Lewis earlier. His brother was his closest friend throughout life, and they were raised in the exact same circumstances. They received virtually the same education, and no parental preference was ever evinced. Yet C. S. Lewis achieved worldwide acclaim through his talents, while his brother lived a rather ordinary, unremarkable life.

How is this phenomenon explained? The only way to understand it is to take both sides of the issue at once. In other words, God often uses natural genetic inclinations to bring forth a person's talents. Yet in His sovereignty, He sometimes seems to "zap" individuals with gifts that cannot be explained by genetic background.

Scripture reveals how God occasionally decides to overrule certain conventions. For instance, Old Testament custom gave special privileges to a firstborn son. Yet there were times when the Lord indicated otherwise, to everyone's surprise. Concerning her twins, Rebecca was told, "The older will serve the younger" (Genesis 25:23). The sons of Joseph were similarly switched (see Genesis 48:14–19). If the Lord wants to make an exception to His rule, who are we to argue?

Thus, while your family background is a good place to start looking for your specific talents, you should not make this a limiting factor. God delights in breaking out of the various molds we have tried to put Him into. He may have placed talents within you that have no genetic explanation, and He desires to help you find them and use them.

Talent—and Fame—at Work

Many people feel untalented and perhaps unappreciated because they do not happen to have careers that place them "in the spotlight." Unfortunately, most of us have been educated to think that the truly talented people are artistic, athletic or perhaps intellectually brilliant. So suppose you are a lightning-quick short-order cook, an exceptional mother, a gifted accountant, a first-rate medical technician, an outstanding kindergarten teacher. You may wonder at times if anyone ever notices or cares about the work you do. And you may begin to envy others' capabilities. But Carlyle reminds us, "All work, even cotton-spinning, is noble."

This can be difficult for us in today's society. We all have talent, yet we have different types of talent. Some gifts can catapult us to fame and fortune, while others— equally important—may lead us to quiet paths and supporting roles. Sometimes it is hard to see how our talents apply to our jobs at all. And many times our talents may be known only by God and ourselves. No matter what our gifting, we can certainly impede its growth and usage (as well as make ourselves miserable) by envying the talents we see in others.

Simply put, not every talented person gets to be president! Will Rogers once noted, "We can't all be heroes, because somebody has to sit on the curb and clap as they go by." Indeed, everyone who has found his way to the White House has benefited from the combined talents of many supportive people. Those individuals may be called "Mr. President," but they would never have heard this salutation without the help of others in a wide variety of talent areas.

Last year I spoke to a group of college-age musicians and asked if any of them had heard of James Smyth, Christian Gottlob Neefe or the Abbe Jelowski. Although these were well-educated, career-bound students, none of them knew a single name. Then I asked if they knew of Handel, Beethoven or Chopin. They knew all of these great composers.

Placing the two lists side-by-side on an overhead projector, I proceeded to explain how each of the "unknowns" had had a profound impact on the lives of the three famous musicians. (Smyth was a strong Christian and encouraging friend of Handel; Neefe, a devout musician, was the young Beethoven's beloved teacher; and the Abbe Jelowski led Chopin to Christ.) Soon the faces in my audience began to sparkle with understanding as they realized that the unknowns' lives had been as important as those of the celebrated composers.

The point is clear: We cannot all be Beethovens, but perhaps we can be Neefes. We cannot all be President Lincoln, but perhaps we can be an excellent campaign manager (without whom, Lincoln surely would never have reached the limelight). Whatever job you have, it can be ennobled by excellence as you apply the talents the Lord has given you. The poet Longfellow once commented, "The talent of success is nothing more than doing what you can do well, and doing well whatever you do."

The Old Testament teaches: "Whatever your hand finds to do, do it with all your might" (Ecclesiastes 9:10). The New Testament echoes this principle: "Whatever you do, work at it with all your heart, as working for the Lord, not for men" (Colossians 3:23). You cannot apply your talents fully if you are distracted by envy of others' talents. Every president, CEO or gifted person with an "out front" job is always searching for talented people to serve in a variety of positions with him or her. You will not often lose a job by working hard within your talent area; you may lose many by abandoning yourself to envy.

One of the most successful people I ever knew for using his talents at work was my father. He was a postman for nineteen years and later a postal supervisor. Not very glamorous, we might think. Yet Dad delivered mail with a passion. He constantly reorganized mail routes to make them more efficient. While walking with his mail sack, he loved to spend the hours memorizing the names of every street and customer. He once even helped design a new stamp. My father took the potentially mundane job of a postman and raised it to artistry by employing his talents of creativity, organization and love for people.

My dentist is another such artist. When he tackles a root canal or puts on a new crown, his hands and concentration are that of a master sculptor. Instead of administering a novocaine shot heedlessly, he makes it a challenge to be as utterly painless as possible, carefully moving his hands by infinitesimal degrees. Simply put, he ennobles his job—one not often considered very artistic—by intentionally utilizing the specific talents God has given him.

My purpose here is to begin broadening our definition of *talent*. It is not limited to the more visible gifts and it is not limited by our lifestyles. You probably would not have considered your postman and dentist "talented artists." And perhaps yours do not happen to deserve such a title. But is this due to a mediocre performance on their part, or because you had never thought of anyone who delivers mail or extracts teeth as talented?

There are very few jobs that cannot use some degree of the talent you have. Martin Luther King expressed it this way: "If a man is called to be a street sweeper, he should sweep streets even as Michelangelo painted or Beethoven composed music or Shakespeare wrote poetry. He should sweep streets so well that all the hosts of heaven and earth will pause to say, 'Here lived a great street sweeper who did his job well.'"

As a taxpaying adult in America, you find on the first page of your annual tax form a line labeled *occupation,* on which you tell Uncle Sam what you do for a living. How many different words do you think are printed in this line in America? That is, how many different occupations do you think exist today? Hundreds? Thousands?

A fascinating management report studied *nineteen thousand* different occupations in America. The writers made it clear that this was not an exhaustive study; they purported to have considered only *primary* occupations! Yet every one of these jobs, in order to be performed with excellence and industry, needs people who have diverse combinations of talent.

To look at this in a different way, consider another aspect of this management study. It took each of the thousands of occupations—from homemaker to taxi driver—and, through a series of careful evaluations, placed every job into one of three broad categories:

1. Leadership
   —Supervisors, CEOs, managers, etc.
2. Working with people
   —Clerks, salespersons, doctors, etc.
3. Working with things
   —Mechanics, computer programmers, repairmen, etc.

Obviously, many jobs do not fall exclusively into one category but involve a combination of these descriptions. For instance, a football coach has to be a leader of his players, work with other coaches on a peer level and master many "things"—such as statistics, plays and strategy. You can think of other examples as well.

Today in contemporary society we have a vast assortment of occupations. This was not always the case. In the Middle Ages, for instance, the number of occupations was rather limited: various jobs on a farm/household, soldier, craftsman, merchant, position in the state (from clerk to kings) and in the Church (from priest to popes). Yet even in such relatively simple times, the success or failure of any worker—whether the position was in the limelight or not—depended greatly on the talents that he or she brought to the work, just as it does today. Some things simply do not change.

Divine Guidance Through Our Talents

Ultimately, discovering and using our talents—at work or anywhere else—is one of the most important aspects of what is often called "divine guidance." As followers of Christ, one of our basic duties is to discern

God's will for our lives—as Paul says, to "find out what pleases the Lord" (Ephesians 5:10). Many Christians are aware of this concept for day-to-day matters, praying that the Lord will "direct our steps" through the small choices that we make each hour. Still others will pray for guidance when confronted with a major decision: whom to marry, where to go to school.

Yet many of us do not ask the "macro-questions" of divine guidance: What would You have me do with my life? How can I maximize the time and talents I have to Your glory? These questions seem daunting to us, perhaps even presumptuous. Yet the answers to such large questions can usually guide us through many of the smaller, day-to-day decisions.

When my father was teaching me how to drive, we once came to a "T" intersection with a stop sign. Having to turn either right or left, I asked Dad which way he wanted me to go. "Where are you going?" was his immediate reply. I simply wanted to hear "right" or "left," so I repeated my question. My father's answer was emphatic: "Where are you *going?*"

In other words, Dad wanted me to consider my ultimate destination. This would, in turn, usually dictate the answers to the many "sub-questions" along the way—such as which way to turn at this intersection. He helped me see that every time I plan to go somewhere, my long-term destination has to be kept in mind when making the short-term decisions of left and right turns.

In the same way, every time I need to make a decision at a crossroads in my life, I will certainly seek the Lord for direction. But the answers to most of these "sub-decisions" are usually clear when I look at them in relation to the big picture, that is, the overall course of the life to which God has called me.

How does one find such mega-direction? An important step is to consider the talents the Lord has given you. Imagine a farm where the farmhands are sent out into the fields to work, each with various tools. Would it not seem odd if one with a shovel banged it repeatedly against a tree? Or if one with an ax tried to use it to dig up the ground? Obviously, if you have been given a shovel, you are supposed to dig. If you have been given an ax, chop down a tree. As the poet James Russell Lowell reminds us, "No man is born into the world whose work is not born with him."

If God has given you certain talents, it is rather likely that they have something to do with your ultimate purpose in life. Granted, you may enter seasons when they are placed temporarily on the shelf. Like Isaac on the altar, we may be called to die to our talents and potential. But the general principle remains in place: You have your specific gifts for a divine reason.

Would God send you through life without the proper accoutrements? It is not His nature, as revealed in Scripture, to do so. The Bible promises us our needed provisions when we are in the Lord's will to do His work. And this includes provision of the necessary talents.

Too many times we beg God for a greater provision of *money* and forget the wonderful provision He has already put within us. It is encouraging to recall the words of Martin Luther on this subject: "Riches are the least worthy gift which God can give man. What are they to God's Word, to bodily gifts such as beauty and health, or to the gifts of the mind, such as understanding, skill and wisdom!"

Your "Acres of Diamonds"

In the late nineteenth century, a Philadelphia pastor named Russell H. Conwell felt called to found a new university for poor but deserving students. This eventually became Temple University. To raise the stupendous funds needed for such a project, Conwell gave hundreds of lectures across the country, which always included the following true story. He entitled it "Acres of Diamonds."

There was once a farmer in Africa who heard about others making fortunes by discovering diamond mines. These accounts so thrilled him that he sold his farm and began to wander the African continent in search of the beautiful gems. But after many unsuccessful years, he became deeply discouraged. Finally, in a fit of despair, he threw himself into a deep river and drowned.

In the meantime, the man who had bought the farm toiled the land faithfully. One day he was crossing the stream that ran through his property and noticed a large "piece of crystal." He brought it home and placed it on his mantelpiece as a curiosity.

Some time later a friend from the city visited the farmer. Noticing the odd crystal, he hefted it in his hand and examined it closely. Gasping with astonishment, he proclaimed that it was a huge uncut diamond. The farmer could hardly believe this, since he knew that his stream was liberally spread with such "crystals." But it was true.

By now you have guessed correctly that this farm turned out to hold one of the largest diamond mines in Africa. The first farmer had owned *acres of diamonds* free and clear, yet he did not know it. He sold them for a pittance so that he could look vainly somewhere else.

If he had taken the time to study and learn more about his area of interest, he might have recognized diamonds in their rough state. And since he already owned a piece of the continent, he should have examined it thoroughly before abandoning it for the unknown. Instead, he became the fool described in Proverbs 28:19: "He who works his land will have abundant food, but the one who chases fantasies will have his fill of poverty." All of his dreams could have come true, but he did not see the diamonds that God had placed all around him.

You, too, are the owner of "acres of diamonds," though you may not be aware of it. The Lord's gifting placed within you is as valuable as jewels and, given the right care, can bring you abundant rewards and fulfillment. Before we make the mistake of trying to imitate (or envy) the talents of others, we have a responsibility to find, cultivate and use for the Lord's glory the gifts already within us.

In the next few chapters we will learn to recognize our diamonds while they are still in their rough state. Like the second farmer crossing his stream, we too may find serendipitous discoveries. We will explore the God-given plot of land that is our inborn talent and uncover those gems that can be cut and polished to perfection.

To Consider and Discuss

1. Have you ever considered yourself "untalented"? What was it that made you feel this way?

2. Consider your family and upbringing. What factors were present that might encourage or discourage your budding talents?

3. Were there obvious talents in your parents, grandparents or other relatives that correspond to the talents you have?

4. How does Russell H. Conwell's "Acres of Diamonds" story relate to your life?

two

What Is Talent? And What Are *Your* Talents?

Whatever you do, whether in word or deed, do it all in the name of the Lord Jesus, giving thanks to God the Father through him.

Colossians 3:17

I once took a fascinating course called "Spiritual Gifts" taught by Dr. Earl Morey, the distinguished theologian who founded the YWAM School of Biblical Studies. As Dr. Morey brought out hundreds of interesting aspects about such spiritual gifts as leadership, teaching and evangelism, I and the rest of the class became spellbound. Being the only trained musician in the course, I could hardly wait to hear all he would have to say about music.

You can imagine my disappointment when the course finally concluded without Dr. Morey mentioning a word about music. I thought to myself, *There is a great deal in the Scriptures about music! Why wasn't it covered?* Having sought out the teacher, I asked him about this omission. His answer was simple. Dr. Morey said, "Music is not a spiritual gift. It is a talent."

Talents Are Natural Gifts, Not Spiritual Gifts

All too often we can blur the lines between important concepts. Dr. Morey was correct: Music is not a spiritual gift. It is a talent, that is, a *natural* gift.

This is a vital distinction, one that is often missed by many writers and speakers today. If music (or any other natural talent) were a spiritual gift—such as evangelism or prophecy—one would surely find that the greatest musicians were all believers. For instance, I do not think there are *any* evangelists among the unbelievers of the world (that would be a strange fellow indeed), yet there are many great musicians.

Spiritual gifts, as listed in the New Testament, are for believers. They always involve a measure of faith to be manifested. On the other hand, the natural gifts we call talents have been distributed to all people, both believers and unbelievers. Unlike spiritual gifts, which are given to those who come to faith in Christ, God rains talents "on the righteous and the unrighteous" (Matthew 5:45).

Why is this distinction important? Because of the different ways we are to consider spiritual and natural gifts. For instance, Paul tells us to "eagerly desire spiritual gifts" (1 Corinthians 14:1). But we are never told to *desire* talents. They are placed within us from birth. Either we already possess them or we do not and never will. Nor should we desire any others than the ones we have—they are plenty.

We saw in the last chapter the futility of envy regarding talent. Thousands of people spend their lives in misery, wishing they were as talented as others around them. In his *Introduction to the Devout Life,* Francis de Sales gives us the most appropriate response to this: "Do not wish to be anything but what you are."

In other words, one's prayer should not be: "Lord, please make me into a better guitarist." That is not the way God generally works with talents. Our job is to discover the talent He has already placed within us and work diligently to improve on it. Perhaps a more biblical prayer would be: "Lord, please help me to practice the guitar with discipline and consistency." Then, if you have within you a God-given talent for playing guitar, such disciplined practice will bring forth abundant fruit. If you do *not* have any degree of inborn talent, then practice will help . . . some. But you will never be a great guitarist.

This is the simple truth and should be accepted as such. The sooner we discover our true talents and stop desiring talents we do not have, the better for all of us. So, if the guitar is enjoyable to you and a blessing to your family and friends, by all means keep playing—but be real about your gifting. Your true talent may lie elsewhere.

Talents Are Inborn, Not Learned

One of the greatest forces of music education in the last century was started by a Japanese violinist named Shinichi Suzuki. He had a beautiful vision to bring music to young children and he personally taught hundreds of youngsters the joy of playing music. Suzuki's many disciples have now made his work a worldwide phenomenon and have helped to nurture the talents of some of today's professional performers.

Yet one tenet within this notable movement is not sustained by the teachings of the Bible. It is the Eastern philosophy—believed by some (not all) Suzuki teachers—that considers a newborn baby a "blank slate," which must then be written upon by the baby's family, environment and society. It states that talents are not inborn but can be learned by hard work and careful instruction.

Such philosophy would proclaim, "Anyone can learn the violin!" Well, sort of. It is true that anyone, with enough work and good instruction, can learn to play some pieces on the violin—yes, even you! But it is perfectly clear to music teachers everywhere that some students have more inborn talent than others. That is, if two students work equally hard on the same piece, the more talented one will always come out ahead. The Scriptures teach that "we have *different* gifts, according to the grace given us" (Romans 12:6, emphasis added). I believe that this is true of natural as well as spiritual gifts.

Should the less talented student quit? Not at all. The job of any student is simply to hone whatever talents he or she has, not to become the "world's greatest violinist"—or scientist or photographer.

But all such honing of our talents has a price: It takes time, considerable effort and usually a lot of money. As French novelist André Maurois correctly asserts, "He who wants to do everything will never do anything." Because of the usually preeminent need in our society to provide one's income, priorities have to be set. It may be that the lesser talented violinist will someday lay aside the instrument in order to hone those areas of greater talent.

This is precisely why it is so important to discover (as soon as possible) the talents we actually have and stop wasting our resources on areas in which we have little. We have a finite amount of time, effort and money that we can devote to perfecting our talents. Let's use such resources well.

What *Is* Talent?

What exactly is this magical stuff called *talent,* which enables some of us to learn a sonata in a day when most of us would take weeks or months or forever? A good, concise dictionary defines *talent* as "a special, natural ability or aptitude." Let's look at these key words *special, natural* and *ability/aptitude.*

1. Our talents are certainly special, since different talents are given to different people. That much is simple.

2. As we have already seen, talents are natural gifts. They come from God, but so do *all* gifts, natural and spiritual. He places talents within us as naturally as He gives us the color of our hair or eyes. We do not have to ask for them any more than we would ask God to give us an appetite for food. He has already done so.

3. And talents are manifested as abilities or aptitudes. In this we see that our talents are not to remain dormant or undiscovered. They are placed in us for a purpose. Jesus said to "let your light shine before men, that they may see your good deeds and praise your Father in heaven" (Matthew 5:16).

In short, our talents were given to be discovered, perfected and used—not to be hidden under a basket. If you, the reader, are already aware of your particular gifting, you may want to proceed to the second section of this book (chapters 4 through 6) to begin the honing process. The rest of us will begin the search. And digging within ourselves, with the help and guidance of the Lord, is like digging in a deep vein of pure gold.

Discovering Our Talents

How do we discover our talents? Most of us have various opportunities to do this as we are growing up. A parent or teacher notices that we do something well and compliments us. Perhaps we win a prize in some area or make consistently good grades in a certain subject. From such seemingly insignificant beginnings we often find direction for our entire lives.

It is a sad fact, however, that many of us did not have caring parents and teachers, win prizes or make good grades. Many of us brought home average (or worse) report cards from school. Some of us were called names—even by our families—that we have never forgotten. It is painfully difficult to believe you contain inborn talent if your friends or family have called you "stupid." Such memories make it a challenge to believe God's infallible Word about you, instead of the fallible words of the people who should have been encouraging you.

Two questions I like to ask school-age children are:

1. What is your favorite subject at school?
2. At which subject are you best?

It may surprise you to find that young students will often give two different answers. They will say, "Oh, I get A's in math but I really like science," or "My favorite subject is history, but I'm better at English." Older students often answer both questions with the same subject, presumably because they have begun to identify their talents in that area. But for the younger students, there are two answers.

Comparing the two different answers of children with the pursuits of their later lives would make an interesting study. I have no doubt, from observation, that the subjects in which children excel point in the same direction as their principal talents or careers as adults. Their "favorite subjects" generally take a backseat as avocations or hobbies.

This is, of course, one of the basic purposes of education: not to fill us with facts and figures, but to allow us to sample a wide spectrum of areas and find which best suits us. As Henry Ward Beecher put it, "Education is the knowledge of how to use the whole of oneself."

For many of us, the subject or interest in which we excelled also became our favorite thing to do when we were young. We enjoyed the outward awards and accolades of our success, as well as the inner satisfaction of mastering a specific area of life. But this was in childhood—and many could not turn this early success into a lifetime pursuit.

The result?

Millions of people are deeply frustrated. They hate their jobs or school, and they feel unappreciated and unfulfilled. And yes, they may be born-again Christians, have beautiful families and supportive churches. Yet they are depressed and discouraged because they do not know the joy of using their talents as God meant them to be used. The great American writer Richard Wright points this out with painful precision: "Men can starve from a lack of self-fulfillment as much as they can from a lack of bread."

Many factors contribute to such frustration, such as sickness, family or marital problems, financial or time pressure, difficult coworkers and a host of other "outside factors." But these usually serve to exacerbate the inner problem; they are not the root cause. The real problem is a failure to use their talents—and, thus, to find their true places in the world in which God has placed them.

Are you one of these? Then you, along with the majority of people who are struggling in this painful area of their lives, fall into two broad categories:

1. *Situation A:* These people, *in their youth,* found areas of talent and fulfillment. But they have been unsuccessful at bringing these experiences into adulthood. They may have been the quarterback on the high school football team, the well-respected editor of the yearbook, the best flutist in the band or the finest actress in the school play. But all that was "a long time ago," now just memories of better days. They were not able to make a living as an adult doing anything related to the talents they found in their youth.

2. *Situation B:* These are the thousands of people who, through no fault of their own, have never been able to discover their primary talents. Again, there are many diverse possibilities for this. Perhaps they received no encouragement as children. Poverty, sickness and other handicaps may have been obstacles. Perhaps they were given a certain talent that was ignored or rejected in their particular environments. For whatever reason, they have never felt talented or found the place God has for them.

The remainder of this chapter will work with the people of *Situation A.* The next chapter will focus on those who find themselves in *Situation B*. I hope that some points from each chapter will be helpful for all readers.

Situation A People

Situation A people are all around us. You are not the only one. They come from every background, rich and poor, urban and rural. Perhaps their one basic commonality is that they feel life has passed them by. They remember that they were more successful, popular and fulfilled in their youth than they are today.

Many former athletes fall into this category. They recall scoring points or winning races and especially remember the roar of the crowds. But no one is roaring approval anymore. Old trophies and faded photographs are collecting dust. Words from Thomas à Kempis' *The Imitation of Christ* come to mind: "O how quickly passes away the glory of the earth." *Situation A* people feel that nothing in the future could possibly compare with the triumphs of the past. And life without expectancy is truly sad.

I remember watching the Olympics a few years ago when a sixteen-year-old gymnast gave an electrifying performance and won the gold medal. It was remarkable and the crowd went wild. Yet I could not help but think, *Here's a girl who, at the young age of sixteen, has probably reached the greatest accomplishment in her life. Chances are she'll never have such a moment to compare with this again. I hope she can handle the comedown.*

Granted, many former athletes and performers handle the comedown quite well and move on to live productive, well-adjusted lives. But there are others who haunt places like sports bars, always looking for someone to tell of their former glories.

This syndrome is certainly not limited to athletes. Consider the thousands of talented young people who hold degrees in history or theater (to name just two), only to find that for every hundred graduates there is only one paying job. What do they do? After tiring of starvation, they usually accept whatever job they can find to pay their bills. Their high hopes and dreams are dashed and they often pine in discontentment. As Scripture says, "Heartache crushes the spirit" (Proverbs 15:13).

Again, there are too many scenarios to recount, but you get the idea. For *Situation A* people, the lightbulb came on at an early age but faded out later—leaving the talented person both disillusioned and unfulfilled.

If you are one of these individuals, don't give up. You can move in the area of your talents! Here are the first two steps in the process.

Step One: What Were Your Talents?

If you can identify yourself as a *Situation A* person, you are already making progress. The first step in solving any problem is to identify it. You are already far ahead of the many people who are downcast but have no real clue of what is wrong.

Let's take a trip back into your past. This may be somewhat uncomfortable for some, but the ultimate purpose is to relieve the frustration of the present. What exactly were those talents that used to be such a part of your life?

Before you answer, first identify two things that are often so tangled they are difficult to separate.

    1. What were your intrinsic *talents?* (Not your ego needs.)

> 2. What *made you feel good* about using these talents?
> (Here is the place for your ego needs.)

Let me explain. All of us have ego needs. This is nothing to be ashamed of, as long as it is kept in its biblical place. For instance, we all have a need to be appreciated and valued. There is nothing wrong with this; God made us this way. This need can be met in a biblical manner (such as displaying servanthood and unselfishness toward others) or in an unbiblical manner (such as craving attention and showing off).

Take, for instance, our example of a young athlete winning a race and hearing the roar of the crowd. If you have such memories, you need to separate your actual talent from the ego need. Hearing a crowd roar its approval of us certainly can make us feel good. But right now it is the talent itself that we are interested in, the raw talent that gives the runner pleasure even if he made the same excellent time by himself on the track without a crowd to cheer him.

To use another example, a musician certainly feels good when he or she performs in public and is rewarded with applause. But the actual talent exists just as much in the practice room when no one else is listening. We need to separate the love of music—or sewing or woodworking—from the love of public acclaim.

Let me explain something that may look contradictory at first glance. Earlier in this chapter the verse was quoted in which our Lord commands us to "let your light shine before men" (Matthew 5:16). Talents are given to us for many reasons, and one is to share them with others. Many of us have talents that we perform before an audience—and this is God's plan for us: to edify others and to bring glory to Himself. But if you as a performer (artist, teacher, public figure) are to "shine your light" as God's servant, then you must make an honest distinction between edifying an audience and meeting your own ego needs.

The reason you need to separate these two has to do with your future, not your past. For if your past contained the fire of a certain talent, you may be able to blow on the ashes and cause it to flame again. But of course, the cheering crowds will probably not reappear.

So let's now concentrate on the talent itself. What were those talents that you discovered and enjoyed in your past? Once you have thought of them, continue with the next step.

Step Two: What Are Your Transferable Talents?

There are two basic ways to answer this question. The first has to do with your *underlying* talents. To illustrate this concept, let's take a case in point.

Suppose you were once an outstanding quarterback. You were probably skilled at throwing a football with great accuracy or running with strength and speed. Since such skills involve a rigorous and precise use of the physical body, you may have lost these abilities by middle age. There are no professional quarterbacks in their forties!

Now let's set aside these obvious physical skills and instead consider the underlying qualities of a great quarterback. They might include quick decision making, the ability to inspire others and a courageous instinct for timely risk taking. These are talents in themselves, whether one uses them to lead a football team, a business, a home or a classroom.

In other words, when trying to rediscover the gifts that you used successfully in your past, look for the underlying talents that may be transferable to your present (or future) situation. For example, if you were successful academically, you probably have talents in writing, communication, accounting or research—which you can use as an adult with great satisfaction. Many of the underlying skills we displayed in our youth are tremendously in demand in the adult world today. And it brings great fulfillment to put these underlying talents to use.

Now let's consider the second way to answer this question of transferable talents. That former quarterback may, in middle age, be unable to throw a football with the same accuracy of his youth. But he may be excellent at showing a young person how to do it.

This has to do with the broad subject of teaching, which includes such related topics as mentoring, coaching, inspiring, training, writing, speaking and tutoring. In other words, the talents of the past may qualify us to train others today who possess similar talents. This may take any route from becoming a college professor to coaching a Little League team. And it is perhaps the ultimate expression of what we have learned. As British writer Samuel Johnson explained, "He has learned to no purpose, that is not able to teach."

This is often an obvious use of talent for those who excelled as young people in the vigorous use of the physical body. Many young athletes turn to coaching, young soldiers later man desks as high-ranking officers and ballet dancers start their own dance studios in order to teach. Long after the human body is unable to perform at its peak, our experience and training can be used to help others reach their potential.

A word here to the spectator who never becomes involved beyond turning on the television. While there is nothing wrong with periodically enjoying the exploits of youthful talent, an exclusive life of this—without taking what we have and giving it to others—is a tragic waste. We need to find ways to give back to those around us, as Jesus' own words point out: "It is more blessed to give than to receive" (Acts 20:35). If you know your area of talent, consider becoming involved with those who share it.

When my children were little they wanted to play on soccer teams, this being the sport greatly in vogue at that time in our area. Unfortunately, there were not enough coaches forthcoming who were experienced in soccer, and I was finally recruited. Although I had played quite a bit of football, my childhood was completely devoid of a soccer ball. As I tried (not always with success!) to keep at least one step ahead of the kids, I often wondered, *Where are all the parents who have a soccer background and can certainly do a better job of this than I?*

After all, when we were young we had teachers, coaches and mentors inspiring us to reach for the heights. Can we not "repay" them by likewise helping the next generation in our areas of talent? And if we did not have these exceptional individuals in our lives, think what it would have meant to learn from someone who shared our passion. Henry Adams, an American historian, said, "A teacher affects eternity; he can never tell where his influence stops." By teaching talented youths, we continue the tradition in which our talent areas have been used for centuries.

This concept is true of all talent areas, not only those that involve the "physical" talents of the past. You may be a writer, an artist, a gardener or a cook—all these gifts need to be taught to the next generation. Is there a way to share your expertise with those around you? In our busy world, many children have only "tried their talents" on video games and movies. Your involvement could create a true legacy, whether you are teaching in a Sunday school class or in your own backyard.

And, of course, this use of our talents is not limited to working with young people. Many adult organizations from rehabilitation centers to senior citizen homes welcome qualified tutors who can help the residents develop their skills. Do you have an interest in poetry? Flower arranging? Carpentry? Your transferable talents will not only bring you fulfillment but can help enrich the life of someone else.

Moving from Spectator to Participant

If you are a *Situation A* person, perhaps you have now thought of examples from your past in which your talents were successfully employed. Perhaps you have now made the second step of identifying transferable talents that could be employed today, either in your profession or in a rewarding avocation. But what about the critical step of putting this into practice? Why does this seem so much easier in theory than reality?

Again, this may have to do with meeting (or not meeting) our ego needs. A talented young ballerina is cheered and applauded, but a ballet teacher—often underpaid and working with many not-too-talented young dancers —may not receive such applause. The basketball star who has taken his transferable leadership skills to start a small business may still miss the thrill of the crowd's cheers.

Yet these individuals can still be fulfilled in employing their talents as God created them to. Thousands of talented Christians in every period of their lives have found tremendous gratification and accomplishment by using their talents for Christ—sometimes even when no one else knew about it.

Note the key words in the previous sentence: *for Christ.*

This is precisely why this book was written, to show how to use your inborn talents for Christ. I have to admit that this may or may not mean using your gifting to make money or to receive applause or even to get recognition. These are the typical rewards that the world offers for the successful use of your talents. If this is what you are after, you may have bought the wrong book. But if you want to know the joy and fulfillment of giving back to God the gifts He has given you, then read on.

This does not mean that the use of your talents will never be appreciated by others—far from it. But it may mean a complete change of attitude. Consider the experience of George Washington Carver, one of the world's greatest botanists: "When I was young, I said to God, 'God, tell me the mystery of the universe.' But God answered, 'That knowledge is reserved for me alone.' So I said, 'God, tell me the mystery of the peanut.' Then God said, 'Well, George, that's more nearly your size.' And he did." This humble Christian man became the world's top authority on the extraordinary value of the peanut and was well rewarded for his brilliant work. But it had to be done God's way.

For each of us this means that we must consider our talents as given for God's purposes and *not as a means of meeting our ego needs*. Frankly, not many adults experience the rare opportunity of having all their ego needs met through applause for their talents. A few of the top movie stars, perhaps, but not most of us. Furthermore, there is nothing in Scripture to indicate that the Lord promises fame and fortune (or even recognition) to all His followers.

Nevertheless, all of us can (and should) find fulfillment in using our specific gifts for Christ. Indeed, this is God's will for every believer. Let's examine how this can be done, both for those of *Situation A* and also *Situation B*.

Talent: A Vertical Relationship

One of the key aspects of Jesus' parable about the talents is the dialogue between the maker and the servants, the giver and the receivers. You will notice that there is no dialogue among the three receivers. They do not compare their different talent levels, at least not with each other. We are left to wonder if they even knew each other at all.

The relationships in this parable are vertical, not horizontal. That is, the relationships given are between the master and each of his servants, but not among the three different servants. This is not an accident of storytelling. It illustrates an important principle concerning your own talents: They are primarily between you and God—not between you and man.

It is the foolish reversing of this principle that has caused confusion and frustration everywhere, including within the Body of Christ. The subtle message (sometimes not very subtle) we have been sold by the world is that unless we receive acclaim for our talents *from other people,* then we are failures. This is utterly unscriptural. Jesus warned His followers repeatedly not to seek recognition from man (see Matthew 23:5–7).

Several pictures portray the concept of this "vertical" relationship. It is not the soprano giving a magnificent concert in front of a huge audience, but the choir member in a lonely practice room day after day. It is not the famous university professor whom hundreds crowd around to hear, but the mother who is endeavoring daily to find new and better ways to teach her children. It is not the White House economist at a press conference, but the faithful bookkeeper who works behind the scenes to keep her company's books in impeccable order.

Please realize that this is not meant to condemn those who happen to be in the spotlight. If God has so ordained it, then He will bless the use of talents in this realm. This *is* meant to define clearly what talent truly is and what we are to do with it. The six people mentioned in the previous paragraph all have talent and all use their talent. Three of them happen to be recognized publicly for it and three of them do not. But this recognition is *not* the talent itself. It is something different, which may or may not be "layered onto" the life of a talented person.

In the fourteenth chapter of Luke's Gospel, Jesus tells of people who are trying to "get in the spotlight"—in this case, to take the best seats at a feast. Our Lord tells us not to be concerned about such matters and instead to "take the lowest place" (Luke 14:10). Public recognition of one's talent is never to be striven for, and it is seldom an accurate gauge of whether we are truly successful or not.

Let me give an example to illustrate what a faulty gauge recognition can be. This very afternoon I served on a board helping to adjudicate a concerto competition at our MasterWorks Festival, the winner of which will perform in concert with our orchestra. All of the young musicians played well, but two violinists offered an interesting contrast.

One was a young man who was not as advanced as the others. It was the first time he had been in a serious competition. I am sure that he did not expect to win but wanted to see if he could simply make it through the event without panicking. He actually did very well and played with a confidence that I think surprised even him. He did not make it past the first round, but the experience of playing successfully in the competition was a great accomplishment.

The other violinist, a bit older and with far more natural talent, made it to the finals. She seemed to be certain she would win, but her performance was rather uninspired. The judges all agreed afterward that this incredibly gifted musician could have won the contest easily if she had simply put her heart into it. She took second place.

This second violinist received more recognition than the first one, who was dismissed after only the first round. Yet one might say that he was more successful at fully using his talent than the second-place winner. Again, recognition by others is not a very reliable gauge.

Our Talents As Offerings to God Alone

This is particularly important for *Situation A* adults. For many of you, your present frustration is not really the inability to use your talents. It more likely comes from the feeling that your talents are no longer recognized and appreciated.

What should you do about this? Unfortunately, many people (including believers) make one of two poor choices. Either they accept their situation grudgingly— becoming depressed or bitter (maybe both)—or they refuse to look at reality and choose to live an illusion. Those of the latter category are the ones in church choirs who always claim the solos (to everyone's horror) or insist on making a banquet for the holidays when others would rather go out. As Goethe commented dryly, "Nothing is more terrible than ignorance in action."

God has a better option. We need to look squarely at the reality of our situations, but we must find a way to do this without depression or bitterness—even if our talents are neither praised nor appreciated by others.

How? Once we understand the "vertical" relationship of our talents and recognize that we should strive for God's approval rather than man's, then we must learn to see our talents as an offering to God instead of an

offering to man. The Bible commands this repeatedly:
"Offer yourselves to God" (Romans 6:13). Our talents
are best employed when they are dedicated completely
to God—when we realize that they come from Him
freely and when we offer them back to Him freely,
whether anyone is around to notice or not.

The idea of laying our offerings before God is, of
course, prevalent throughout the Bible, and the Old Testament practice found its fulfillment in the sacrificial,
atoning death of Jesus Christ. Yet, while we can dispense
with certain types of offerings, such as burnt offerings
and wave offerings, we do not discard the concept of
offering every part of our lives to the Lord. This image
fits perfectly with the correct use of our talents.

Picture yourself offering your talent completely to
God without any other person nearby. Now compare
this with a portrait of a Jewish high priest offering a
lamb or a bull. Both offerings came from God and are
now freely given back to God. The offerings are made
to the Lord and not to man (though man may partially
benefit from them). In both cases, no comparisons are
to be made as to *the amount* one person may have to
offer over another: God accepted equally the massive
offerings of King Solomon and the small offerings of
the poor. God is pleased to receive both offerings, if they
are made with pure hearts.

If we are to use our talents to glorify the Lord, then
we must "un-learn" certain worldly values. We must see
that the chief reason God gave us talents is not to bring
us money, fame or recognition. Talents were given *primarily* so that we might have a glorious means of praising Him, as we offer our gifts back to their source.

Situation A people: What were your talents? For
most of us, we still have them, at least in some quantity. Let's forget about using them to bring the rush of
excitement that came when we were once lauded by

our peers. Instead, let's offer them daily to God. Let's use them at every opportunity, even if no one else ever knows about it.

An outstanding example before us is Johann Sebastian Bach (1685–1750), universally considered to be one of the greatest composers ever to have lived. This Christian musician cared nothing for the praise of men. He worked most of his life in small churches, writing his masterpieces for rather obscure audiences. Of the hundreds of compositions he produced, only ten were published in his lifetime. It was seven decades after his death that Bach's genius was finally discovered and appreciated. Yet it did not matter to him; he was composing for the Lord. He ended many manuscripts with the bold letters *S.D.G.,* Latin for *Soli Deo Gloria* meaning "To God Alone Be the Glory."

Our Lord will always delight in our gifts, even if others do not. God is not a critic who will disparage or belittle our abilities. James describes the Lord as one who "gives generously . . . *without finding fault*" (James 1:5, emphasis added). He would rather hear the quavering voice of an elderly woman singing praise than the most accomplished unbelieving singer in the world (or even the most accomplished *believing* singer who is not using her talent to glorify God).

And why not? On man's scale, a vast distance seems to exist between the abilities of the two singers in the preceding sentence. But the Creator of the universe is so far above any of our human talents that on His *infinite* scale there is little difference between the talents of a beginner and a Caruso. As C. S. Lewis reminds us in an article about church music: "For all our offerings, whether of music or martyrdom, are like the intrinsically worthless present of a child, which a father values indeed, but values only for the intention."

As for you *Situation B* people, let's now take these principles and expand on them, that you might find your undiscovered talents and offer them to the Lord.

To Consider and Discuss

1. What were your favorite subjects as a youngster in school? How did these change as you matured?

2. What do you consider to be your primary giftings? Are you using them regularly?

3. Do you consider yourself a *Situation A* person? That is, did you once have talents that you are no longer using? Or are you a *Situation B* person?

4. Do you have talents that might be transferable to your present situation? Explain.

three

Discovering Your Unknown Talents

I have filled him with the Spirit of God, with skill, ability and knowledge in all kinds of crafts.

Exodus 31:3

There is an old story about a preacher who, while driving through the countryside, came upon a beautiful farm. Its crops were in well-ordered rows, the fences were in good repair and the freshly painted house was surrounded by trees and gardens. As the preacher stood admiring the sight, he noticed the farmer coming toward him as he plowed a nearby field. The preacher waved to him and shouted, "My son, God has blessed you with a wonderful farm."

The farmer stopped plowing and wiped his brow. He remarked, "Yes, sir, He has, and I'm mighty grateful." Then he thought a moment and added, "But y'know, preacher, you should have seen the place when He had it all to Himself!"

This humorous tale contrasts two important aspects of our Christian walk: our responsibilities and God's responsibilities. Our lives are like that farm. God placed within it tremendous potential, and for this we should be indeed grateful. Yet it will never bear fruit without our own efforts. The most fertile farm in the world soon becomes only acres of weeds without a diligent farmer.

In the same way, God has put amazing talents within each one of us, but it is our responsibility to discover them, work on them and bring fruit from them. In the previous chapter we saw how this discovery process can unfold in the lives of *Situation A* people. Now we shall consider how to uncover talents for *Situation B* people—those who have never thought of themselves as particularly talented. This same process will show each of us how to realize previously unknown talents that may lie within.

Situation B People

If we acknowledge that God has given *everyone* talents, we have to consider the odd position of the *Situation B* people. Millions of individuals today have never been considered particularly talented, either by themselves or anyone else. Of course, this does not mean that they are impoverished or unsuccessful. Many have good jobs and often earn high wages. But they feel that they are simply accomplishing tasks set before them by others. They rarely experience the joy of fulfillment that comes from using their finest talents. English satirist Jonathan Swift put it this way: "It is in men as in soils where sometimes there is a vein of gold which the owner knows not of."

If the talents are really there, then what is the problem? They are like the farmer's field "when God had it all to Himself." That beautiful farmland was just as fertile and valuable when it was still covered with thorns, weeds and briars—but no one could tell by looking at it. This illustrates the principle found in Proverbs 25:2: "It is the glory of God to conceal a matter; to search out a matter is the glory of kings." Before that farm's value could be revealed it had to be "searched out," and a great deal had to be cleared away from it.

In the ideal situation, this "clearing process" took place in our youth. Parents, teachers and friends collaborated informally to help us try different areas of endeavor, to find those in which we excelled and to encourage us to develop these skills. But, as we have noted, for many of us, this did not take place.

Can it take place now? Is it still possible for adults to discover talents within them? Of course. It can be difficult. As adults, we may not have the free time we had as youngsters. There may be no one nearby to encourage us. A lack of external praise may dampen our motivation.

Nevertheless, such obstacles can be overcome. A myriad of adults have learned to play the piano, paint landscapes, write books and do hundreds of other things with competence that they never learned in their youth.

For example, the famous painter "Grandma Moses" (Anna Mary Robertson Moses) was a farmer's wife who began painting in her late seventies—and created more than sixteen hundred works! A painting of hers exhibited in a drugstore window was seen by New York art critic Louis J. Caldor, and the rest is history. She used to say, "If I hadn't started painting, I would have raised chickens." The great French painter Henri Rousseau did not start painting until he retired from the army. His new talent fulfilled him for the first time in his life:

"Nothing makes me happier than to contemplate nature and to paint it." Rousseau gave us many renowned works including *The Sleeping Gypsy*, *The Happy Quartet* and *Jungle with a Lion*.

In a different vein, Harland Sanders ("Colonel Sanders") found his true business talents at age sixty-five when he began franchising his well-known Kentucky Fried Chicken restaurants. And of course, a certain Ronald Reagan, after many years as an actor, developed his inborn talent as a statesman. He served as governor of California and then president of the United States, both for two terms.

Thousands of adults have discovered talents that were unknown for decades. Socrates began the study of music when he was eighty. Golda Meir became prime minister of Israel at seventy-one. And Benjamin Franklin, after dabbling in a variety of occupations, accomplished his most important work for the infant United States after he turned sixty.

But first, they had to find their talents.

The Clearing Process

Before your own ground can be cultivated, planted or fertilized, it first must be cleared. In the "clearing process" for discovering unknown talents within you, a number of steps should be taken in the proper order:

1. Preparing mentally and emotionally
2. Examining universal possibilities
3. Reviewing your past experiences
4. Examining specific possibilities
5. Experimenting with new opportunities
6. Receiving counsel and instruction
7. Evaluating your new gifts

We will look at each step in detail in this chapter. But first let me stress the correct *order* of these steps. All too often we try to initiate something new in our lives in a haphazard manner, with few results. Perhaps we jump into a new idea without any preparation or without proper counsel. Or we try to evaluate a situation long before it is time. At any rate, our best results will come with an approach that is orderly and measurable.

1. Preparing Mentally and Emotionally

Last week our orchestra at the MasterWorks Festival was led by renowned conductor John Nelson. The works on the program (by Beethoven, Sibelius and Dvorák) were compositions he knew thoroughly and had conducted many times before. Nevertheless, for two hours prior to the concert the maestro secluded himself in his room and would not be disturbed. It was not to study the music but simply to prepare himself mentally and emotionally for the performance.

For any challenging task such preparation is essential. As Abraham Lincoln once said, "Your own resolution to success is more important than any other one thing." This is not referring to daily, practical preparation, but an additional effort that precedes the event itself. An athlete, for instance, will work hard in preparation for a championship match. But in addition to regular practice, he will also "psych himself up" days ahead for the challenge before him.

Before you plunge yourself headlong into the task of discovering inner talents, you need to prepare for this process. You need to determine within yourself that you are "in for the long haul" and will not quit when times are difficult or confusing. Rome was not built in a day, and the discovery and honing of one's talents does not take place in a day. The outcome will be worth the effort.

It is not unusual to talk with someone who says something like, "I've always wanted to become a writer." But a few questions quickly disclose whether this wish is a serious desire or merely a whim: "Have you begun to study the craft of writing?" "Do you have a collection of works by great writers?" "How much have you written *this week?*"

Jesus admonished us to "count the cost" before we begin a project lest we be ashamed of being unable to finish it (see Luke 14:28–33). Take a moment to pray before going forward. Prepare your heart and mind for the task ahead. Remember to pray about this every day, asking for God's help and direction. Determine not to give up in a day or week or month. For if you fully resolve to achieve the goal of finding and using your talents for Christ, find and use them you will!

2. Examining Universal Possibilities

Many books related to the topic of talents cover this step rather exhaustively. They present long (often very long) lists of possible talents, sometimes covering every activity a human can perform on this planet! Maybe this is to suggest a few potentially achievable goals, like "hangnail removal," for even the most ungifted reader.

An easier approach is to consider all human talents in broad categories. Then we can explore areas within these categories to find previously undiscovered gifting within us. Look through these categories, listed below, in the same way an experienced miner might study a site that interests him. Do not be discouraged if nothing jumps out toward you immediately; you can explore in detail later. Remember: Many a miner has had to move tons of dirt in order to find a gold nugget!

Consider the following twelve categories of God-given talent. They are not given in any particular order; no specific gift is more important than any other.

Artistic talents
Leadership talents
Communication talents
Athletic talents
Research talents
Mechanical talents
Organizational talents
Counseling/relational talents
Tactile talents
Teaching talents
Social talents
Intellectual talents

It is certainly possible to name a talent (perhaps a rather obscure one) that is not covered by these categories. Nevertheless, these twelve divisions of natural talent cover a vast array of possibilities, and you need to consider each one carefully. As you read the next several pages, you may want to keep your finger in this one, in order to revisit the list and examine how each category may or may not affect your life.

3. Reviewing Your Past Experiences

To some degree, you are at this moment the sum total of all the experiences you have had in your past. That is, every experience that God has sent you has had a part in shaping how you act and think presently. Perhaps you like chicken soup because it brings back warm memories of your childhood. Or perhaps you detest chicken soup because you had to eat it so often as a child! Either way, your background has created your present tastes.

Yet there is more to your present state than simply the sum of all your past experiences. For inside each of us are talents that are yet to be discovered, and therefore they have yet to create new experiences for us. They are like books sitting on your bookshelves that have never been read, or seeds stored in packages that await planting. How are they best discovered? By reviewing your past to find connections that can point to future possibilities.

Here is an example. "Alice" is a discouraged *Situation B* adult who has never felt particularly talented. She may have a degree, a job, a husband and children, but she has never known fulfillment in the areas we are now considering. Perhaps she has been reading this book and is now convinced that she must truly have been given some degree of talent. As she ponders this truth, a resolution to seek out her God-given gifting deepens within her. Montaigne once asserted that "We are born to inquire after truth"—and now Alice is ready to begin her search.

After examining the twelve talent categories listed above, she prayerfully examines her life, asking God to reveal past experiences that may point to talents she has never realized. When Alice ponders the word *counseling,* she recalls that as a child she was always the member of the family who acted as referee between battling siblings. Not that Alice has ever been a formal counselor or has even thought of herself as one. Yet she remembers that even in her neighborhood, she was usually the one who could coax two fighting friends into talking and eventually playing again.

Why was this talent never explored when she was younger? A thousand reasons may be possible. Perhaps Alice's parents strongly encouraged a completely different direction for her. Perhaps a friend she admired happened to comment disparagingly of those who counsel. Perhaps someone once told her that only men should be counselors. Who knows? But for one reason or another, Alice never explored this path, never planted and cultivated these seeds to see if they would grow.

Now she is ready to try again. She is determined to explore once again her potential in Christ. And the more she ponders her past experiences, the more she is convinced that she indeed possessed a relational gift that has never been developed. She seeks God's direction and begins to picture herself as a counselor, seeing in her mind's eye the many different ways she might help others in this manner. Alice is starting to live out the maxim given by Goethe: "Before you can do something, you must first *be* something."

This is an important step and should never be minimized. Scripture insists that we should never despise "the day of small things" (Zechariah 4:10). Though Alice still has a long way to go in order to make this dream become a reality, she is ready to keep moving forward. What is the next step?

At this point you, like Alice, may have narrowed the field of universal possibilities in keeping with your own experiences. Now it is time to examine the specific possibilities within your own life.

4. Examining Specific Possibilities

If you are ready to begin, you need specific direction. You may know where you want to go—just as Alice wants to explore her possible gifts as a counselor—but you do not know how to get there.

Here is the next step. You will need prayerfully to write—and probably rewrite—four separate lists. This is a difficult task for many, but you must trust that God will lead you into His will through this exercise of faith. Just as the Lord commanded Habakkuk to "write down the revelation and make it plain on tablets so that a herald may run with it" (Habakkuk 2:2), so you and I need the same written clarity.

Therefore anyone in Alice's situation must sit down at a computer or with a pad of paper and write the following things:

A. *What I need to know*—Make a list of everything you need to know about your talent goal but do not know at this time. Such a list might include questions like: "Do I need to go to college for this?" "Are there certain books I should read?" "Can my pastor help me with this?" Do not be afraid if this list grows quite long. It is far better to see what needs to be done than to stumble on without a clue about your needs.

B. *Whom I need to know*—This is a list of people who may be able to help you on your way. Your list may include specific names. Alice, for instance, may already know a counselor or have a friend who once went to a counselor. Your list might also contain such entries as "college professor," someone you need to meet with in order to obtain more information.

C. *All known obstacles*—Before an obstacle can be conquered it must be identified. Maybe you live in an isolated region. Maybe you have never met anyone related to your talent area. Be as specific as possible. For instance, do not list "money." Find out *how much* money is needed for books or courses, then put that amount on the obstacle list. It is much easier to pray for (and work for) something specific than for an immeasurable abstraction.

D. *My plan of action*—Now you must go into high gear. You must slowly construct a list of specific steps, based on the needs represented in the first three lists. When possible, include dates for action. If the first list contained certain books to read, then this list must include a date for purchasing or borrowing them and a proposed date by which they should be completed. If the second list mentioned certain people to meet, this one must show when they will be contacted. Finally, each obstacle on the third list should have a corresponding item on this list. For example, if a sum of money is needed, then your list should indicate how and when it can be worked for and saved.

Let me stress that these are long-term projects, not short-term "to-do" lists. They will neither be written in a few minutes nor completed in a few days. Some steps may take months or even years to finish. Remember that while it can be a daunting task to find new talents in your life, the rewards are always worth far more than the effort. Just thinking about these steps can add a new and positive dimension to our lives. Samuel Johnson once said, "Few moments are more pleasing than those in which the mind is concerting measures for a new undertaking."

Nevertheless, for some of us such long-term planning can be disheartening. Do not despair! When I begin an extensive project I try to remember this: "The end of a matter is better than its beginning, and patience is better than pride" (Ecclesiastes 7:8). Now we see the supreme importance of step one: inner preparation for the journey. As I mentioned earlier, such prayer and pre-paredness become an *ongoing* step, as we ask the Lord daily for help and encouragement.

5. Experimenting with New Opportunities

Now it is time to get out of the house and try a few new things. It is not necessarily the end of planning (course-correction will be another ongoing process), but it is the beginning of doing. It is the time actually to per-form the various tasks that have been written down on your plan of action.

What will *you* be doing? Well, everyone's talent and aspiration is different, so everyone's plan of action will also be different. Alice may make an appointment to see a local counselor and find out more about what is needed to become one. She may purchase a number of books to read or register for courses to attend. But she will begin *doing* something—probing, experimenting, exploring—not just dreaming about it.

For instance, if you are attempting to discover an artistic talent, you may begin to take lessons on a cer-tain musical instrument, try out for a small part in a local drama company or sign up for art classes. What-ever your talent area, people are presently working in it and they can and should be contacted. You have to start somewhere—and the sooner the better.

For many of us, all this can be rather frightening. Frankly, any time we are venturing out of old patterns we are taking a risk. We may fail. We may be embar-rassed. Things may go wrong. If you are feeling less than confident about this, don't condemn yourself. German writer Jean Paul Richter reminds us that "courage con-sists, not in blindly overlooking danger, but in seeing and conquering it." With God's help, your fears can be conquered.

There is really no way to try something new without the possibilities of failure. Again, to use the analogy of mining for gold, a miner knows that when he begins digging in a new vein he may be wasting his time. He may dig there for weeks and find nothing. But if he never ventures to dig anywhere, he is guaranteed never to find the gold. The only guaranteed failure is doing nothing!

The Bible says to "cast your bread upon the waters" (Ecclesiastes 11:1)—in other words, *try things*. Not everything we try will be successful, but nothing can ever be successful unless it is attempted, unless the risks are recognized and accepted. We must trust the Lord to guide us through such uncharted waters and to give us courage to step out of our comfort zones and attempt something new.

Incidentally, you will notice that the ideas I have mentioned have more to do with study and preparation than with actual performance. That is, if you decide that you have a knack for interior decorating, you should possibly take classes in design and architecture. You should *not* volunteer to redecorate the parsonage. (Gulp!) As I mentioned earlier, we often get a new idea and rush into it without the proper preparation, only to be frustrated and discouraged. True, we need to be doing and not just dreaming—but we need to be doing the right things. (More on this in the next three chapters.)

6. Receiving Counsel and Instruction

There are really two parts to this step, which are represented by the two words *counsel* and *instruction*.

By *counsel* I mean that in the midst of all your exploring you need to seek out a few trustworthy people to give you counsel and advice—not professional counsel, but a few wise friends, family members or your pastor who will be *very* honest with you about your new ideas. This should be someone who knows you quite well and whom you trust enough to believe, even when he or she says something you do not want to hear.

Let's face it. Sometimes we get some pretty strange ideas, supposedly in the name of the Lord. I thank God that I have a few close friends who love me enough to rebuke me when needed. It hurts to hear it, but "faithful are the wounds of a friend" (Proverbs 27:6, KJV). I have found that when I think one way and all my closest friends think another way, then usually I am wrong and they are right. That is a good general rule to follow. This is why Scripture says that "plans fail for lack of counsel, but with many advisors they succeed" (Proverbs 15:22).

So before you attempt a tryout for your local professional hockey team or begin sousaphone lessons, run the idea by someone you trust. Again, to quote Montaigne: "It is good to rub and polish our brain against that of another." You can tell if your friends are really with you or simply being polite. If they think you are crazy, they may be right. Ask why they feel as they do. Then take this back to the Lord in prayer, asking for direction and clarification.

Incidentally, they may think you are crazy and they may be wrong! Counsel is important, but ultimately this is between you and God. I have not often gone against such counsel given me, but if I believe that I have to, I had better be certain of God's guidance in such cases. As always, there is no substitute for seeking the Lord.

Concerning *instruction,* I refer to those persons from whom you may seek professional instruction in your new talent area. Whether it be a college professor or a private teacher, there is no use going to him if you are not prepared to *submit yourself* to his teaching. This can be especially difficult for adults, particularly if the teacher is younger than we are!

When we were children we were sent to teachers all the time. We may have been good students or poor ones, but we realized ultimately that our teachers knew more about the subject matter than we did. Yet as adults, we have already achieved confidence in many areas and it can be rather humbling to assume a student role again. Furthermore, since we are now used to learning things quickly, to start a new area at the beginning can truly be a trial of patience (or lack thereof).

My first teaching experience was as a high school student when I taught a guitar class for children a few years my junior. I quickly found that there were two types of students: those who wanted to learn the guitar and those who simply wanted to *play* the guitar. Those of the second category really did not want to work through the learning process; they wanted to magically (and instantly) be able to play this difficult musical instrument. As you may guess, those students never did well with the guitar. But the others worked hard, slowly and faithfully, and eventually became fine guitarists.

As you begin this wonderful new process, guard your heart. Approach it with humility, patience and fortitude. Be content with taking one small step at a time. Demosthenes taught that "small opportunities are often the beginnings of great enterprises."

7. Evaluating Your New Gifts

Let's suppose that our imaginary friend Alice has now been moving in the direction toward counseling for some time. She has met with two professional counselors for advice, has read a number of books on the subject and is now taking a correspondence course. She is even considering a major step, such as enrolling in a nearby college. It is time for some careful evaluation.

By this point, Alice has (we hope) learned two important points:

A. She has learned a great deal about "the world of counseling." That is, she has a fairly good idea about the daily life and work of a professional counselor and the type of materials and skills needed.

B. She has learned a good bit about herself and, specifically, whether or not she really has the talent, inclination and energy needed to continue in this direction. She is finding out if this idea is a serious possibility for her life.

Now Alice stands at a crossroads. Like anyone at such a lifetime crossroads, she needs to spend time daily in prayer and Bible reading, seeking the Lord for confirmation.

Suppose she continues in the counseling talent area. Does she have a guarantee that God will bless those efforts? I am afraid not. But, of course, she does have a promise that God will never leave or forsake her (see Joshua 1:5).

Suppose she turns back and abandons her counseling efforts. Was it all in vain, a waste of time and energy? Certainly not. Sometimes in our zeal to hurry from one thing to another, we forget that all productive learning is good, that the Bible insists, "It is not good to have zeal without knowledge" (Proverbs 19:2). Such a learning experience for a growing Christian is wonderful. It makes us more complete, increases our possibilities for service and makes us all the more "ready to do whatever is good" (Titus 3:1).

And suppose she stays at the crossroads. That is, suppose she never takes college courses and becomes a professional counselor, but neither does she abandon her efforts. Instead she continues to read and sharpen her skills to the point that she can be a valuable counselor for her friends, in her church or in many other informal settings. This is a worthy use of her talent. Helen Keller once stated an important truth: "I long to accomplish a great and noble task, but it is my chief duty to accomplish small tasks as if they were great and noble." This may indeed be God's perfect will for Alice and the counseling talents He has given her.

One should not begin trumpet lessons, only to later consider himself a failure if he does not become the next Louis Armstrong. One with tactile skills does not have to aspire to be the world's greatest brain surgeon; he may instead become a fine gardener. That is to say, any crossroads at which we find ourselves may contain any number of possibilities. When evaluating a new step to take, always be sensitive to the multitude of options the Lord may have for you.

As we discover and perfect our talents, let's remind ourselves constantly *why* we are doing so: for the glory of God alone—and for whatever service (great or small) He may deem to give us to bless others. For the Bible reminds us again and again: "Whatever you do, do it all for the glory of God" (1 Corinthians 10:31).

To Consider and Discuss

1. Which of the twelve talent categories do you believe includes you? Think of incidents in your past to support this.

2. Consider the possibility of exploring a new talent area. Can you list what you need to know about it, as well as any known obstacles?

3. What about a plan of action? List a few things you now intend to do, and note when you intend to do them.

4. Name two people you trust to give you wise and truthful counsel in this area.

Part 2

Perfecting Your Talents

four

Improving Oneself

It is required that those who have been given a trust must prove faithful.

1 Corinthians 4:2

The next three chapters deal with topics that are all too often left out of books about talent. That is, most books related to this subject are concerned only with finding one's talent and using one's talent. But the critical stage that exists between the act of finding and the act of using is ignored. I am referring to the stage of perfecting one's talent, improving on it, making it worthy to be presented, both to God and to man. This use of the word *perfecting* brings to mind the picture of a knife being honed to a fine edge; the Lord would have us sharpen our God-given skills to their highest potential.

It is the omission of this supremely important topic that results in much of the mediocrity we observe today. For some reason many of us seem to think that our raw, newly discovered talents are immediately ready for public consumption. It is not uncommon to see someone who has just begun singing get up in front of a smiling (but miserable) congregation, or someone who has recently purchased water colors create a painting they would like hung in the church lobby.

Jesus told us that "a student is not above his teacher, but everyone who is *fully trained* will be like his teacher" (Luke 6:40, emphasis added). Unfortunately, some would like to skip the "training" part and move on to public use of their talents. It simply does not work this way.

A good analogy to the three-stage process of finding, perfecting and using our talents is that of preparing a main dish. First, a cook discovers a new recipe and gathers the needed ingredients. Then comes a time of preparation, often quite lengthy, involving chopping, measuring, mixing and, of course, cooking. Only after this is completed do we have the final stage of presenting the dish to those who will enjoy the resulting delicious food.

With this analogy in mind, we might say that those who neglect to hone their talents before openly presenting them are like a cook who serves unwashed vegetables, uncut pineapples and uncooked meat!

Mediocrity Within the Church

At the risk of sounding scornful, I simply must state that this lack of preparation is notoriously prevalent in the Church today. Indeed, you are probably already aware of this regrettable situation, perhaps from examples in your own church. We have all known people—wonderful, Jesus-loving believers—who are in church positions they could never have garnered in the world. Speakers with little or no training, leaders of committees without the needed people skills, musicians who know only a few notes—the list could be extended *ad nauseam.*

Someone may counter that "none of us is perfect." This is certainly true. I have worked with some of the world's best musicians, and they will be the first to admit they still miss notes. But they try hard every day not to! Yet, believe it or not, many people seem to consider self-improvement efforts to be almost anti-Christian. Augustine analyzed the situation correctly: "It is human to err, but it is devilish to willingly remain in error."

Rather than dwell further on this deplorable state-of-the-art-of-the-Church, I ask the simple question, Why? Why on earth has the Church—of all places!—become the asylum of so much un-talent, or at best, un-preparation? And why do we put up with so much of it?

There are good reasons and bad reasons.

The good reasons have to do with the audience or, rather, the congregation. Yes, God calls us to be long-suffering, to encourage one another, to abstain from complaining and to avoid hurting each other. If I am in the congregation, therefore, when either an untalented or an unprepared singer is howling, it is my Christian duty to be patient, smile and quell any critical spirit that may arise in my thoughts. Such Herculean efforts can be character-building.

The bad reasons have to do with the howler, not the congregation. I am afraid that this howler *also* knows that God has called the congregation to be longsuffering, to encourage one another, to abstain from complaining and to avoid hurting each other. The howler can get away with murder, therefore, without facing justice. No matter how badly the howler howls, there is no danger of a well-aimed tomato or the time-honored "Boo!" Instead, smiles (or at least, patient silence) and perhaps even compliments venture forth. Such well-intentioned praise actually perpetuates the problem by inciting another appearance next Sunday!

In other words, we Christians have a bad habit of taking advantage of one another. We think to ourselves (one would hope that this is an unconscious thought), *They are Christians, so they will forgive my sloppiness. They have to, right?* Granted, we should realize that most of us have indulged in this error from time to time. I will admit sadly to performing in front of congregations with much less preparation than I would have given to a Kennedy Center concert. And I have, as a minister of music, sometimes allowed others to do the same— rather than love them enough to work with them or to steer them to different roles.

The Parable of the Talents: Behind the Scenes

But this is never the attitude Christians should cultivate concerning our talents. Our duty is to take whatever talents we may have and *improve* on them. We should strive for excellence at all times, whether performing for a few friends or on national TV, whether before an audience of thousands or alone with the Lord.

Let's examine a somewhat neglected aspect of the Parable of the Talents found in Luke 19:11–27. As you recall, the story takes place in two separate periods of time: the day the master gave out the talents to the three servants, and then the day when he returned and demanded an accounting.

But what about the interval in-between? It is all too easy to pass over it and proceed to the end of the story. We do not know how long the master was away; nor does the Bible expound on this portion of the text. The final result, however, does tell us something important about this time period, however long or short it was.

The first two servants presented their master with a greater amount of talents when he returned. Did this happen by magic? Did they somehow find these new talents along the roadside? Of course not. The obvious implication is that these two faithful servants *worked* their talents, knowing that they were called to improve on their present situation. Indeed, the third servant was rebuked because he did not attempt to do this.

Proverbs 14:23 tells us, "All hard work brings a profit, but mere talk leads only to poverty." If we are to use our talents for the Lord, we must expect to work diligently. The great evangelist Charles Finney used to say, "Sweat plus sacrifice equals success," and he was right. Thomas Edison gave us another good word on this subject: "Opportunity is missed by most people because it is dressed in overalls and looks like work."

As we have seen in the preceding chapters, we all have been given talents. Therefore, we must now decide which of the three servants in Jesus' parable we want to emulate. And one of the fundamental differences between them was how much they were able to work and improve. In other words, we begin improving our talents by improving ourselves.

"Isn't This Just a Worldly 'Self-Help' Idea?"

Many Christians have difficulty understanding this concept of improving oneself. It sounds too similar to the "self-help" teachings prevalent throughout the secular world. But take note of the important differences.

The worldly version of self-improvement leaves God completely out of the picture. It is called "self-help" because it is "self-oriented." It lies to us: "You can do it! You have the power within you!" Some are even more dangerous, making vague references to "spirits" or getting you in touch with your "inner self."

The most powerful lies are those that contain a portion of the truth, and "self-help" is no exception. The truth is that we should each improve ourselves. The lie is that we can do so in our own strength, and furthermore that we are to do so for our own benefit. This does not come from God's Word. Yet the truth remains that we are called by the Lord to improve on what He has given us, with His help and for His glory.

Another objection some Christians make might hark back to the hymn title *Just As I Am*. They ask, "Doesn't God love me just as I am? Why do I need to improve myself? Doesn't the Bible teach that we are saved by God's grace, and not by works on our part?"

Yes, of course it does. We are not now referring to eternal salvation but to the stewardship of one's present life on earth and how to maximize it for Christ. Certainly God loves us just as we are. By improving ourselves we are not trying to merit His love—which is utterly unmerited and "unmeritable." We are simply doing as He instructed so that we may serve Him better.

Jesus told us, "From everyone who has been given much, much will be demanded; and from the one who has been entrusted with much, much more will be asked" (Luke 12:48). If you have been given talent (and each of us has) then He does not want you to "hide it in the ground" but to work with it, improve on it. As Paul says, "It is required that those who have been given a trust must prove faithful" (1 Corinthians 4:2). Our talents are trusts from the Lord, and we must prove faithful with them. Someday, like the servants in the parable, we will have to give account. Have we multiplied them, expanded and improved on them? Only then will we be commended: "Well done, my good servant!" (Luke 19:17).

How Can I Do a Better Job of What Christ Has Given Me to Do?

The above question is one that we should ask ourselves frequently. We should not only think about it, but it should be a matter of sincere prayer. Since God desires our improvement, He will always make Himself available to help us. We are not in this alone! A good prayer is: "Lord, help us to serve You—as well as those around us—better today than yesterday."

In fact, this applies as much to our devotional lives as to our business or family lives. For instance, every year I want to learn to pray with greater potency, to worship the Lord with deeper intimacy, to know His Word with wiser understanding. Surely we can all agree that such improvements are in the will of God!

A friend of mine has been with Wycliffe Bible Translators for many years and has already made a complete New Testament translation in a foreign language. This devout man of God once gave a powerful sermon I will never forget. He admitted that, although he had two master's degrees and was working on his doctorate, it occurred to him one day that he was reading his Bible *the same way he did in high school*. He began to pray for improvement in this crucial area, and it radically changed his life—and the lives of many others.

If you are saying, "All right, but didn't Jesus teach us to come to Him like little children?" (Matthew 18:3), yes, indeed. We should always nurture a heart of humility, meekness and personal modesty. But this does not condone apathy and impassivity to learning. Paul sets the perfect balance when he commands, "In regard to evil be infants, but in your thinking be adults" (1 Corinthians 14:20). Even as we improve ourselves for Christ, we must remain humble and submissive, which is, incidentally, the best state for any kind of learning.

Renowned Christian writer G. K. Chesterton taught that "true contentment is the power of getting out of any situation all that there is in it." For many of us, such efforts are difficult and we find ourselves discouraged by how much improvement we still need. It is then that we should heed the words of Francis de Sales: "Do not lose courage in considering your own imperfections, but instantly set about remedying them—every day begin the task anew."

Take an example from the everyday world. Suppose you are a talented auto mechanic. Are you a better mechanic today than you were five years ago? What are you planning to do that will make you an even better mechanic in five more years? Obviously, you will have more experience—and this is certainly important. But what are you doing, outside the typical daily workload, to become better at your profession?

A friend of mine is a skillful mechanic and has saved me large amounts of time, hassle and money over the years. He reads everything he can find on the technology of the newest cars. He regularly attends classes on related topics. (Being a musician, I have no idea what he really does.) My friend is already considered a master mechanic, but he never stops learning—and neither should we.

Lifetime Learning Is a *Biblical* Principle

Lifetime learning is a concept that may be new to many of us. Some people, when they are graduated from college or high school, think to themselves, *Whew! Now I've finally paid my dues!* But the growing Christian never takes this attitude. His or her life can be pictured by the beautiful Proverb: "The path of the righteous is like the first gleam of dawn, shining *ever brighter* till the full light of day" (Proverbs 4:18, emphasis added).

Look at any living thing. If a plant is not growing, then it is ultimately dying. Once an animal ceases to grow, it begins developing the first signs of old age and death. There is simply no place for standing still. This principle applies to all of life. This is the way God made the universe. Who are we to argue? In the same way, if we, as Christians, refuse to learn and grow at *any* time in our lives, we become less useful to the Master.

Of course, there are many different types of learning and growing. Some growth is *quantitative,* such as the natural growth of the human body. Other growth is *qualitative.* This cannot be seen with the eye, but is taking place within us every time we learn, improve our skills and gain wisdom from above. It is qualitative in that it brings higher quality of life and service to us and positively affects those God has placed around us.

The point is that some growth (that is, improvement) must be evident in our lives or we are dying. As writer Harvey Ullman reminds us: "Anyone who stops learning is old, whether it happens at twenty or eighty. Anyone who keeps on learning not only remains young but also becomes constantly more valuable."

Certainly, no one can grow in every direction at once. There are different seasons in our lifetimes in which we concentrate on certain areas and set aside the others for subsequent attention. Don't feel guilty if you are unable at this time of your life to improve your major talent. Perhaps that can begin at a later date. But in the meantime, what *are* you able to learn? What areas in your life can be improved? It is thinking along these lines that will make us "ready to do whatever is good" (Titus 3:1).

Many verses admonish us "to grow" (see 1 Corinthians 3:6; Colossians 1:10; 2 Thessalonians 1:3; 2 Peter 3:18). Often, in our quest to be spiritual, we forget that *growth* does not refer simply to the supernatural aspects of life but also to the natural life. In other words, God wants us to grow and improve in *every* area of life, from our quiet times to our businesses, from our family lives to the use of our talents. This is true for Christians of all ages, as Scripture exhorts: "Teach a wise man, and he will be wiser still" (Proverbs 9:9).

Money in the Bank *v.* Too Many Withdrawals

At this point it might be helpful to explain more fully this concept of improving oneself. Specifically we need to distinguish between a true honing of one's talent and the mere outward appearance of it. Many well-meaning individuals are going through the motions of improving, yet the results are nil—or even getting worse!

One of my closest friends, Jim Kraft, an excellent trombonist in the National Symphony Orchestra, tells his students, "Practicing is like putting money into the bank; performing is like taking money out of the bank."

You see, many inexperienced musicians think that as long as they are playing their instruments (whether in practice or performance), they are improving. This is not true. Performing will not help you play better; only practicing will help you play better. Indeed, if someone performs frequently but never practices, he will not stay the same—he will regress.

I know a musician who had played in a major orchestra for more than twenty years. One day he decided not to practice any more. He reasoned (correctly) that he had spent his life playing his instrument, that he was one of the country's finest players and that he had certainly played the entire repertoire many times over. All this was true. Yet after three months of rehearsals and performances without private practice, his conductor gave him a warning notice. His colleagues in the orchestra took note weekly of his musical regress. The warnings had no effect in motivating him to practice again. Three months later he was fired.

How could this be? Six months earlier he was considered by all to be a world-class performer. But his "bank account," without any deposits of practice, was quickly emptied. Only in private practice can a musician improve, not in public performances. Only in private practice can a musician correctly listen to himself, critique his work and slowly try things that encourage improvement.

Now apply this analogy to your particular talent and you will find that the concept is always borne out. Each of us must regularly work *on our own* if we want to improve. It is not the times of public applause that hone our skills. We improve best in the private time we invest consciously answering the question *How can I make this better?*

A few questions to ponder: Are you better today at (your talent area) than you were this time last year? Why? That is, what did you do to make this happen? What worked to help you improve? What are you presently doing to make certain that you will be better next year at (your talent area) than you are today?

Praying or Thinking About Your Talent—Or Both!

It is obvious to anyone who has read the Bible that God desires every Christian to pray. We are to pray not just in church or in times of great need but "continually" (1 Thessalonians 5:17). We learn to see prayer in its highest potential: not merely as importuning the Lord for assistance but as a means for ongoing, intimate relationship with our Father.

Prayer is truly one of the most important parts of our Christian walk and the last thing I want to do is discourage you from praying. But so much emphasis has been placed on prayer that many believers seldom get around to another private activity that God desires for each of us: *thinking*. Let me explain.

If we are going to improve ourselves, we need to spend more time *thinking*. And you are now saying, "I think all the time—in fact, all day long." But I am afraid that the type of thinking I refer to seldom occurs in any of us. As Isaiah states in disgust, "No one stops to think" (Isaiah 44:19)! You see, it is quite possible to get through a day's activities with little or no real thinking. You may react to stimuli around you, and you may remember to perform routine actions. You may even make many decisions—yet you never indulge in one of the greatest actions you can do with the brain God gave you: think.

By thinking, I mean that you stop what you are doing, concentrate on one subject or problem that must be solved and force yourself to come up with new ideas and solutions. The best way I know to think is with a blank piece of paper (or computer screen) in front of me. Perhaps I have a certain problem to solve. I discipline myself to think in a focused manner until I come up—not with one answer—but with ten to twenty possible answers.

How does this relate to our talents? No matter what our talent areas are, if we are to improve on them we must learn to improve ourselves by thinking better. The famous playwright George Bernard Shaw said, "I think I'm rich and famous for thinking a couple of times a week." We must constantly find solutions to the many obstacles before us. But do not just think of one answer, think of a dozen. The best answers usually come after prolonged thought. And the best way to get a good idea is to get *a lot* of ideas—one of them will be good!

So, what about the Scriptures like Proverbs 3:5 that says to "lean not on your own understanding"? A marvelous answer to this was given by the great Bible teacher Howard Hendricks. While exhorting his students to use their brains for Christ, he explained: "The Word says to 'lean not' on it, but it doesn't say not to use it. Just don't lean on it!" In other words, we need to use the best thinking apparatus we have, always realizing that it is still small compared to the wisdom and guidance of the Lord. We were given brains to think with, and we must be good stewards with them and consciously *think* more every day.

An excellent variation on this concept is called *brainstorming*, that is, thinking creatively in a group setting. This can be especially beneficial when you are getting together with others who share your talent area. It is wonderful (and powerful) when talented people who are trying to improve their skills come together and ask collectively, "How can we do this better?" Ideas start flowing and new ideas are built on old ones. The results can be inspiring for all.

Incidentally, the best thinking sessions I ever had were those well blended with fervent prayer. Ask God to lead you in your thinking. Prayerfully consider each idea as it comes to you; bring it before the Lord. Scripture uses many different words for this idea *(ponder, meditate, consider),* but they all encourage us to use our brains for Christ. Praise God for the fantastic gift of thinking!

Your "Two People"

Some years ago it was popular for Christians to wear a button with the following letters: *P.B.P.W.M.G.I.N.F .W.M.Y.* These were the initials of the words *Please be*

patient with me; God is not finished with me yet. When
this secret message was decoded for someone who
asked, it usually generated a smile and perhaps a nod
of agreement.

When most of us hear the sentence, *God is not finished with me yet,* we often think in the negative. That
is, we translate the phrase into something like "God is
still *cleaning me up.*" And He assuredly is—as we let
Him. All of us carry some negative baggage that needs
to be left behind.

But can we turn this around to the positive improvement of our talents? One of the reasons that "God is not
finished with me yet" is that He is still helping me
develop the gifts He has placed within me. God and I
are on a journey together. But it is not simply a journey
of repetitive plodding; it is a sojourn of daily advancement, enrichment and transformation. The Bible states
that we "are being transformed into his likeness with
ever-increasing glory" (2 Corinthians 3:18).

Here is a good way to picture this concept: See yourself as two people. One is your present state up to this
moment, including the state of your talent level. The
other is you in, say, a dozen years, and the vast improvements you have made with the talents God gave you.

Imagine a man standing erect, with another—and
much larger—man standing behind him. The larger
man represents the incredible potential of those who
accept the discipline and sacrifice needed to improve
what they now possess. Right now, all you (or anyone
else) can see is the smaller man. But God sees the greater
man He has called you to be, and He will work with you
on the journey toward your potential in Christ. The
words of the great writer George Eliot should always
ring in our ears: "It is never too late to be what you might
have been."

Do you remember the Old Testament story of Gideon? (See Judges 6–8.) Usually we recall his great triumph, when he bravely destroyed Israel's enemies with a vastly reduced army. Yet the beginning of the story shows that Gideon was not always so brave. In fact, when the angel of the Lord appeared to him, he was doing his work in hiding and answered with timidity and insecurity (see Judges 6:11–15).

Yet note, at Gideon's inauspicious beginnings, the greeting of God's angel: "The Lord is with you, mighty warrior!" Gideon could only see the little man that he presently was, but the Lord saw the greater man standing behind him—the intrepid warrior we now remember him to be. We are often like Gideon on that day, looking with fear and disapproval at our present unpromising circumstances. But God sees what we can become.

Input *v.* Output

GIGO is a term that computer programmers sometimes use, which stands for "garbage in, garbage out." When we say that we have powerful computers that can do amazing things for us, we really are referring to the tremendous skill that a human being used in building and programming the computer. A computer is only as good as what was placed in it. Hence the somewhat comical term "garbage in, garbage out."

Jesus stated this important principle like this: "Out of the overflow of [the] heart [the] mouth speaks" (Luke 6:45). In other words, that which we place into our hearts comes out in our speech and actions. If our hearts are filled with love and humility, then our speech and actions will reflect these virtues. But if we have brought selfishness, anger or greed into our hearts . . . well, GIGO.

This is a particularly important principle in regard to improving ourselves, for the use of our talents can be considered "output" from our lives. The quality of this output will always be in direct proportion to the quality of our input.

For example, let's take two athletes of comparable talent. One of them trains carefully every day, while the other's efforts are haphazard and unsystematic. In other words, their talents may be similar, but they are allowing different *input* into their lives. Each man's resulting output is obvious.

It is this very factor that can enable some of us with lesser talents to compete with the great. Scripture says that "if the ax is dull and its edge unsharpened, more strength is needed" (Ecclesiastes 10:10). Therefore, if our axes are dull—that is, our talents are only second-rate—we may be able to make up for this deficiency with a good deal of first-rate work.

It is this first-rate input that can make all the difference with our resulting output. I heard a famous baseball coach say: "I'm not looking for the 'natural athlete'; I want a guy who will go after the hard ones." And my friend Christopher Parkening, one of the world's foremost guitarists, recently remarked, "Our goal should be to overcome what we lack in talent or ability by what we have in dedication and commitment."

Let's keep it simple. You know you have some degree of talent. You want the use of this talent, your output, to be of excellent quality. Then the answer is to combine your talent with excellent input—that is, excellent training and honing of your skill. The equation is as follows:

$$\text{Talent} + \text{Good Input} = \text{Good Output}$$

Cramming

Let's further consider this "input," the things we must do to improve ourselves. For a businessman it might be keeping up with all the latest developments in his line of work. For a teacher it might be reading books and materials written to enhance the art of teaching. For all of us it means *thinking* a great deal about our area of talent. (We may not be able to work on it every day, but at least we can think every day!) The list might include a hundred things, but it is all input we allow into our lives to work toward our improvement.

In what manner should we garner such input? This is an important question and one that is often ignored. You may see a student studying and, naturally, approve and admire her efforts. But what if she is merely cramming for tomorrow's exam, and the materials will be forgotten by next week? How does the manner in which she studies affect the outcome?

Consider the practice habits of two young musicians. One practices thirty minutes each day. The other ignores practice for most of the week but crams in five hours the day before the weekly lesson. Although the second child actually practiced more that week than the first child, the manner in which he worked did more harm than good. Music teachers can always spot this error as soon as the lesson begins.

The Bible gives us an important principle in Proverbs 13:11: "He who gathers money *little by little* makes it grow" (emphasis added). This applies not only to money but also to any way that we seek to improve ourselves— and, thereby, our talents. Rather than slowly and surely working a little every day to improve, we sometimes make the mistake of trying to cram in weeks of work into too short a period. Not only can this be frustrating and exhausting, but it can often hinder rather than promote our improvement.

Shakespeare wrote: "Many strokes, though with a very little axe, hew down and fell the hardest timber's oak." It is the faithful, sometimes infinitesimal details of daily work that lead to self-improvement and allow the Lord to use our talents in this world. Helen Keller once stated: "The world is moved not only by the mighty shoves of the heroes, but also by the aggregate of the tiny pushes of each honest worker."

There are many, many verses in the Bible that include the words *every day* or *day after day.* They refer to doing those things God has called us to do in a regular, consistent manner. This is the way to improve—and to really live! Chuck Yeagar, the test pilot who first broke the sound barrier, was once asked how he became so incredibly proficient at flying—as well as handling the stress of his dangerous job. His answer told the story: "I try to learn something new and have some fun every day."

Improvement One Day at a Time

What is it that you want to improve on? What talent do you possess that needs honing? If you already have discovered your talents, then you simply have to do three things to watch your talent grow:

1. Find what input (activities) will help your talent to grow,
2. Schedule these activities into regular (perhaps daily) periods of time, and
3. Discipline yourself to keep to this schedule.

Let's suppose that you have a talent for writing poetry. Here is how the above list might apply to you:

1. Find what input (activities) will help your talent to grow, such as reading the great poems of English literature, buying books about poetry and its structure, going to seminars and poetry classes, meeting other poets, writing and rewriting poems, and having your work critiqued by writers you respect.
2. Schedule these activities into regular (perhaps daily) periods of time. Perhaps you should read poems or read about poetry for thirty minutes each day and write poetry for thirty minutes each day. You may want to take one writing course each year and go to poetry meetings once each month. As soon as you have written a new poem, you could take it to a local professor for a critique.
3. Discipline yourself to keep your schedule. Get out your calendar and write on it! Place tentative dates for the periodic activities listed above. Determine regular times of your day for the needed reading and writing. Perhaps you should tell someone you trust about this schedule to keep you motivated and accountable. Now go for it!

As I look up from my writing I see a tall brick wall nearby. Every brick is in place, each one bearing its share of the load. None is missing. If there were gaps, broken bricks or missing mortar, the entire structure would be weakened. But the bricks were laid one at a time, and so this wall has stood strong for many years.

Our lives are like this wall, and each day is like a brick. If we build our talents faithfully, a little each day, we will have strong results. If we work sloppily or without direction, the results will not be desirable.

The psalmist prays: "Teach us to number our days aright, that we may gain a heart of wisdom" (Psalm 90:12). We approach our work, practice and perfect it one day at a time. There is no need to worry about tomorrow's honing or to try and do tomorrow's tasks today. As Jesus told us, "Do not worry about tomorrow, for tomorrow will worry about itself. Each day has enough trouble of its own" (Matthew 6:34). Henry Ward Beecher reminds us: "We steal if we touch tomorrow. It is God's."

By dedicating ourselves to improving daily—little by little—we will gradually but surely grow into someone "useful to the Master and prepared to do any good work" (2 Timothy 2:21).

To Consider and Discuss

1. Concerning the concept of lifetime learning, what have you learned in the past year that has helped you in your talent area?

2. How does the picture of putting money into the bank relate to your talent area?

3. What are some ways you can improve your talent this year?

4. Once you know of something new you need to do, what is your plan for adding it to the routine of your life?

five

Building Your Repertoire

He said to them, "Therefore every teacher of the law who has been instructed about the kingdom of heaven is like the owner of a house who brings out of his storeroom new treasures as well as old."

Matthew 13:52

This chapter delves into another aspect of our talents that is too often ignored. Many of us, once we have discovered our talents and honed them a bit, produce something of quality and then immediately expect the world to beat a path to our doors. When the inevitable lack of praise and appreciation hits home, we can become discouraged to the point of quitting altogether. This is due in part to ignorance of the principles of repertoire building.

By *repertoire* I mean the accumulated past experiences, training, knowledge and pertinent ideas you bring to the table that represent you and your talent level. You might think of this as a résumé or vita. An actor's repertoire is the roles he or she has learned or performed. A musician's repertoire is the specific compositions learned, performed and ready to be performed again. A cook's repertoire includes the dishes that have been perfected and can be prepared with confidence.

As our talent areas grow and improve, we must each build solid repertoires. Proverbs 10:14 tells us that "wise men *store up* knowledge" (emphasis added). Thus, while we look with pleasure on our newly created works and praise God for His blessing upon them, still we must not be content there. As we achieve a certain milestone, we should turn our hands immediately toward the next work to add to our growing repertoires. The marvelous composer Franz Schubert lived this principle: "As soon as I finish one work, I begin another."

Quality and Quantity

This emphasis on quantity may not seem to fit at first with the importance of producing something of quality. Remember the adage "Never sacrifice quality for quantity." This is an excellent dictum. We should never lower our standards of excellence in order to crank out more product, particularly with the goal of possibly making more money.

Yet too much of a focus on this dictum can blind us to another important truism: Sometimes the way to achieve higher quality is to increase quantity. That is, if you try something over and over again, you get better at it. If you want to make or do something of excellence, give several attempts and each will likely rise in quality. Anything you do with perseverance and diligence tends to improve.

In the last chapter I mentioned that one way to get a great idea is to get a dozen ideas; one of them will probably be good. The same repertoire-building principle works in a wide variety of areas. If you want to paint a beautiful sunrise, paint scores of them. If you want to write a moving song, write dozens of them. If you want to take a striking photograph, take several rolls of film. Not only will your skill improve, but you will find that different sounds or images will move your listeners in many different ways. But you must first determine to start and to keep going. The celebrated poet Christina Rossetti once commented, "Can anything be sadder than work unfinished? Yes, work never begun."

Beethoven composed *nine* symphonies. I am very glad he did not stop after his first one; indeed, we would never have heard of him if he had. Sir Edmund Hillary and Tenzing Norgay finally reached the top of Mount Everest on their *seventh* attempt. Each previous endeavor brought them a little closer to the summit. Verdi is often called the king of opera. Yet it was not until he had composed sixteen operas that he created a hit, *Rigoletto*. His finest masterpieces were still to come. Suppose he had stopped at opera number fifteen?

Do you know why some popular music groups appear on the scene with a splash but then disappear quickly? They are sometimes called "one-hit" bands. They record one interesting song and jump into the arena, but they have no repertoire behind them. So they go from the "top ten" back to obscurity.

Someone who has spent time building a substantial repertoire is ready when a great opportunity arrives. Long before recording artist Michael Card was "discovered," he had worked diligently at writing songs. At one point, this then-unknown singer wrote a new song every week and performed many of them in his local church. Therefore, when he was finally approached by a record company he was ready. Rather than simply present one hit song, Card had dozens to bring forward—and the record company was more than a little impressed.

Did Jesus give us *one* parable? Not at all. He spoke many parables to illustrate the many facets of His Kingdom. Once, after teaching His disciples about the Kingdom of God, Jesus ended with a picture of a man with a large and valued repertoire: "Therefore every teacher of the law who has been instructed about the kingdom of heaven is like the owner of a house who brings out of his storeroom new treasures as well as old" (Matthew 13:52). The Scriptures admonish us to store up our repertoire of varied teachings and experiences, so that we might "be prepared in season and out of season" (2 Timothy 4:2) to do the Lord's work.

While I was in music school, I privately began an in-depth study of the Bible. Over time, the Lord showed me many incredible lessons from His Word. I started taking notes and keeping a private journal, which I called, "Sermons I'll probably never give." It seemed well named, since, as a young music student, I certainly never thought of giving even one sermon. Yet God had other plans. Now I speak quite frequently, and I do not have near as much time on my hands as I did in college. This journal has been an invaluable source of material for me, and I doubt that I will ever use all of that stored-up repertoire—indeed, it is the source for much of the book you are now holding.

On a Train to Richmond

As a lover of history, I enjoy reading biographies of great men and women throughout the centuries. One of the historical characters I admire is the renowned Christian General Robert E. Lee. And my favorite Lee biography is the Pulitzer-prize winning four-volume set by Douglas Southall Freeman.

Lee's famous accomplishments took place during the American Civil War, and thus his personal history might be divided into three parts: (1) before the war, (2) during the war and (3) after the war. Freeman's huge biography gives a full volume of details of Lee's life long before the Civil War began, when he was an unknown Army officer. One notices in this biography a pivotal chapter, set in time just before the war began, entitled "On a Train to Richmond." In this chapter the author reviews all the obscure jobs, posts and training that Robert E. Lee experienced prior to the war (his "repertoire") and compares them with the monumental events and pressures that were soon to follow.

This before-and-after comparison reveals some amazing facts for those of us who are building our repertoires. For virtually every diverse task the Civil War placed on the general, there had been a specific time of preparation beforehand. It is spellbinding reading as the author skillfully shows how each difficult but thankless task that the young Lee was forced to conquer equipped him perfectly for the struggle ahead. In other words, Robert E. Lee went into the war with a huge repertoire of experience from which he drew as needed.

The Bible states that "a man's steps are directed by the LORD" (Proverbs 20:24). Is this simply a nice platitude or do we really believe it? It is surely one of the most encouraging promises in the Bible. It means that if we are truly trying to follow the Lord, then He will arrange for all types of serendipitous experiences to be added to our lives. In other words, God Himself will help us to increase our repertoire.

When I was working on my doctorate, the dean of the music school asked me to take charge of his publicity and public relations department. I agreed grudgingly and was soon up to my elbows in writing press releases, arranging for concerts and talking to music critics. Let me assure you this was not my idea of fun! Many times I asked the Lord why He had me involved in such drudgery that did not interest me at all. Yet years later, when we started the Christian Performing Artists' Fellowship with dozens of outreach performances, that earlier experience was invaluable to me. I was able to channel what I had learned in graduate school toward doing the work of the Lord. Looking back, I clearly see God's wisdom in giving me such needed experience.

Although we may be working toward many goals (more on that subject in a moment), we really do not know where we will be in, say, ten years. In fact, James reminds us that we "do not even know what will happen tomorrow" (James 4:14). Therefore, we need to absorb all the extra experiences we can along the way, even if we do not yet see the ultimate reason for them.

Advancing on the Many Levels of the Journey

As I mentioned, my wife is a cellist, as well as an outstanding cello teacher. Though she has taught many adults, most of her students are in high school or elementary school. Some start at an early age and continue with her for a number of years. At each weekly private lesson, she carefully guides the student along the challenging journey through the cello repertoire, from beginner pieces eventually to major concertos.

Since I am (mercifully) not present at these lessons, I hear the students only when I accompany them at their annual recitals. (After 25 years of this, I have become an expert in a unique field: piano accompaniment to the student cello repertoire.) How remarkable to chart their progress over the years! Last year one student played a simple arrangement, but this year she performed a Vivaldi sonata. Next year she may play her first student concerto. The order is never haphazard. Each selection builds on the technique learned in the last year's work.

My point is that building a repertoire is a *gradual* process. You do not start a beginner on the Dvorák *Cello Concerto*. Neither do you give an advanced student "Twinkle, Twinkle." One needs to learn in the proper order, improving incrementally to the next level. When this guideline is not followed, the result is usually frustration and demoralization.

Yet it is all too common to have an adult or older student demand to work on a composition that is far over his head. He may attempt it with fortitude, but without the proper techniques learned in other simpler pieces, he will fail. Jesus told us, "Whoever can be trusted with very little can also be trusted with much" (Luke 16:10). Some of us want to be entrusted with much long before we have been faithful with the little. This never works. It takes a long time to master any talent area and a long-term approach is imperative. It helps to pray for patience as well!

The life of David makes a marvelous study of building repertoire slowly but surely. As an unknown shepherd boy, he demonstrated that he could fight off a bear and a lion. Then, as a young man he defeated the giant Goliath. Later, as a commander of Saul's troops he learned warfare and leadership skills. It was only after many years and a variety of learning experiences that he was made king.

The Bible tells us that "there is a time for everything, and a season for every activity under heaven" (Ecclesiastes 3:1). If we are to improve and increase our repertoires, then we must first recognize where we are on the journey. We should take things in their proper order. If

I am a beginner, then I must recognize it and learn accordingly. Even Shakespeare, Mozart and Tiger Woods had to start somewhere. As Emerson reminds us, "Every artist was once an amateur."

"Practice Makes Perfect"

Anyone who has ever been in the music department of a college or university has probably walked by a number of small compartments called practice rooms. There is usually a piano inside, and perhaps a mirror and a music stand, but little else; nothing else would fit! In such unremarkable cubbyholes, thousands of musicians spend hours each day practicing their music and hoping to perfect their skills.

The concept of practicing is valid within every talent area. Some, like ballet dancers, practice in groups. But most talents are best sharpened when we are alone. There are fewer distractions, and we can concentrate on the task at hand and be the first to critique our efforts. Socrates tells us, "If a man would move the world, he must first move himself." Therefore, we must all find the time to practice if we are to advance our skills.

Nevertheless, as we have noted, it is all too possible to spend hours at practice and not advance our skills at all. This important fact is sadly unknown to many aspiring young musicians—and probably to others in different talent areas as well. You see, if a young musician simply goes into a practice room, plays through a stack of music and then leaves, probably no improvement will occur.

In other words, there is a right way to practice—and a wrong way.

What is practice? What is supposed to take place in our practice time? How can we best use our practice time to advance our skills as far as possible? These are relevant questions whether you are a glass blower, public speaker, tennis player or quilter.

I do not know where your specific talents lie, so I cannot give exact practice techniques to you. But I can point out the underlying principles that are behind all practicing and you can "translate" into your talent area.

First of all, the purpose of practicing is to improve our skills, period. This generally involves a lot of hard work and is usually not a lot of fun. It does not have to be miserable, of course, but it is serious business. Proverbs 14:23 insists, "All hard work brings a profit." If we want to profit from our practicing, then it will be through hard work. And enthusiasm for this work will keep us from being discouraged by any failures we might encounter. As Churchill said, "Success is going from failure to failure without loss of enthusiasm."

Please do not misunderstand me. All this talk of hard work should not negate the pleasure of simply sitting down at the piano and experiencing the joy of playing through some lovely pieces. But that is not *practicing,* and it will not improve our talents.

Whatever your talent area, there are four points that should always be present (and repeated) in your practice/learning time for it to be profitable, and these take place in the right order:

1. Know what you are trying to accomplish.
2. Make an attempt.
3. Critique the attempt.
4. In light of this critique, now try again.

These four pillars form the basis of all practice, whether you are a baseball pitcher trying to improve a curve ball or a salesman trying to refine your presentation. Perhaps the most important of all—and the one most often neglected—is the first step. Always begin practicing by knowing what you *want* to do. It is difficult to hit a target if you do not have one before you. This concept of a target, or goal, leads us to our next section.

Prayerfully Setting Goals

Believe it or not, many Christians have grown uncomfortable about the topic of goal setting. Maybe they have run into a worldly version of this biblical idea. Perhaps they have been hurt in the past by insensitive goal setters who lost perspective and considered goals more important than people. Indeed, many strange teachings exist in the world about goals. But avoiding such error should not cause us to abandon the entire concept. As the saying goes, "Don't throw out the baby with the bathwater."

God gives us many examples of goal setting throughout the Bible. When Noah started hammering, his goal was to finish the Ark. When Moses went to Pharaoh, his goal was to obtain release of the Israelites. When Joshua entered the Promised Land, his goal was to conquer it, bit by bit, battle by battle. When Solomon began construction, his goal was to build the Temple. When Nehemiah explored the rubble around the destroyed Jerusalem, his goal was to rebuild the walls. This list could go on and on.

Someone might argue that these men were not trying to accomplish a goal; they were simply obeying the guidance of the Lord. The answer is, yes, of course, because *God gave them these goals!* Our object as believers is not to avoid goals, but to discern what *God's* goals are for our lives and to accomplish them.

When Jesus was determined to go to Jerusalem and His disciples tried to distract Him with a report about

King Herod, the Lord replied: "Go tell that fox, 'I will drive out demons and heal people today and tomorrow, and on the third day *I will reach my goal.*' In any case, I must keep going today and tomorrow and the next day—for surely no prophet can die outside Jerusalem!" (Luke 13:32–33, emphasis added). Paul told the Philippian church: "*I press on toward the goal* to win the prize for which God has called me heavenward in Christ Jesus" (Philippians 3:14, emphasis added).

Such expressions are more than religious slogans. They represent an attitude of striving toward specific and measurable goals. Jesus divided His goal into daily segments and refused to be dissuaded from achieving them. Paul speaks of more than just the goal of eternal life; he is clear about the ongoing goals of his ministry. And so must we be. We must seek God's goals for our lives—and particularly those that reflect our talent areas.

Every goal attempted and achieved is a stepping stone toward perfecting our God-given gifts. Without such measurable goals, it is often impossible to know how well we are progressing on the journey before us. As Seneca put it, "Our plans miscarry when they have no aim. When a man does not know the harbor he is making for, no wind is the right wind."

Goals come in a variety of shapes and sizes. For a pianist, a long-term goal might be to obtain a degree in music. A middle-range goal might be to learn all the Chopin *Preludes*. A short-term one would include today's practice sessions. Each is deliberate and measurable: It is important to know whether one has succeeded or not in obtaining the goal.

Consider your own talent area. What might be a long-term goal to which you can aspire? As to the middle-range goals, these may well have to do with learning or creating an extensive repertoire that displays your skill. The short-term projects are generally those that can be accomplished in one to seven days. But we need goals, plans, targets for which we can aim. Victor Hugo stated: "Where no plan is laid, where the disposal of time is surrendered merely to the change of incident, chaos will soon reign."

Take a moment now prayerfully to establish some basic goals to shoot for. Remember: It is better to aim for the stars and perhaps hit the treetops, than to aim for the treetops and hit your feet!

Course Corrections

There may be those reading this who truthfully admit: "I simply don't know what goals God wants me to have. What should I do in the meantime?" If you are in this situation, there are two things you should do:

1. Seek the Lord in daily prayer for His guidance. Ask God to show you the goals you are to pursue. He may reveal this through circumstances, through specific leading in His Word, through the counsel of those around you or through many other ways. Your job is to seek the Lord.
2. In the meantime, be exploring. Try different things to see what opens up for you. Sometimes the Lord shows His will for you by blessing the situations you attempt. At any rate, this is not a time for sitting. If you stay sensitive to His leading, God can always give you course corrections as you are moving. We need to avoid becoming dormant and to remember the advice of Franklin Delano Roosevelt: "Above all, try something!" You simply cannot steer a parked car!

At first glance this might seem presumptive. You may say, "I should not act until I am sure I have God's guidance. Didn't the Israelites follow the cloud when it moved, but stop when it stopped? Shouldn't I do the same?"

Here lies an important difference. The Lord told the Israelites to go when the cloud moved and to stop when it stopped. But if you are presently seeking direction, then God has not yet told you to stop. (If He does, do so!) You may still be uncertain as to which way He wants you to go, but if He has not said to stop, your job is to "search out [the] matter" (Proverbs 25:2).

In the previous chapter we looked at the beginning of the story of Gideon. God sent an angel to give him the goal of saving Israel from the Midianites. When the reluctant Gideon began to express doubts, the angel gave him six words that we should remember whenever we also have our doubts: "Go in the strength you have" (Judges 6:14).

We, too, should go in the strength we have, inadequate though it may seem to us. A few paragraphs ago I quoted F.D.R.; now I will quote his uncle, Teddy Roosevelt: "Do what you can, with what you have, where you are." Such exhortations leave no room for excuses, but ample room for achievement.

If you do not yet have direction, remember the call of Abraham, when God commanded: "Go to the land I will show you" (Genesis 12:1). Note the changes of tense within this verse. The Lord said "go" in the present tense, yet "I will show you" in the future tense. If we will simply start moving today, trusting Him to give us course directions as needed, God will reveal all we need to know in His perfect time.

Readers Are Leaders

Whatever your talent area happens to be, you are not the only one ever to have explored it. There are likely thousands of other people who have been similarly

gifted, and many who have mastered the field. Therefore, a critical question arises: How can we learn from
those who have gone before?

One obvious answer concerns books. I do not know
what your talent area is, but I am certain that there are
books written about it and equally certain that you need
to be reading them.

Recall Jesus' words: "From everyone who has been
given much, much will be demanded; and from the one
who has been entrusted with much, much more will be
asked" (Luke 12:48). One of the demands on those with
talent is that they learn from others from the same talent area. Whether you are interested in basket weaving
or bungee jumping, there are books written on the subject that contain valuable information for you.

As the old saying goes, "I have bad news and good
news." The bad news is that reading is becoming a lost
art. Even though literacy has risen during the last century, so has dependence on visual media: television,
videos and so on. And the person who does not read is
no better off than the illiterate who cannot read.

The good news is, if you ignore this trend and read
regularly you will have a tremendous advantage over
those who do not. You will learn faster and improve with
a great rate of consistency. And you will enjoy it all the
more!

Obviously we should be reading for pleasure. But we
should also find as much good teaching material in our
talent area as possible. Praise God for libraries! If you
do not have a library card, get one this week. There are
thousands of books that can be borrowed, and if one is
especially important you can surely purchase it at a
bookstore or on the Internet.

Of course, this admonition also covers other learning
aids, such as tapes, library and Internet research, seminars. I never drive anywhere without several books on

tape to hear. It is like reading and driving at the same time! Remember to keep your eyes on the road, but if you happen to become interested in what you are hearing and miss an exit from time to time, it will be well worth it.

Part of building our repertoires is going through a wonderfully long list of recommended reading book by book. A good start is to make such a list yourself and check off each book when it is completed. Furthermore, make a list of the specific materials (such as reference books or research software) that you want to own eventually. Then you can watch your growth and improvement as you watch your personal library grow.

Seek Out People of Wisdom and Knowledge

My father always used to say that everyone should know a good doctor, a good dentist and a good mechanic. Whatever other possibilities you may want to add to this list, the concept remains the same: We need to know many good people in order to live in this world. The Scriptures tell us that "wisdom is supreme; therefore get wisdom" (Proverbs 4:7). A corollary to this principle is that we need to seek out *men and women of wisdom* at every opportunity.

We are (and should be!) mutually interdependent with many others. When poet John Donne wrote "No man is an island," he was not trying to encourage a certain lifestyle or ideal; he was simply describing a fact he had observed. Whenever you pick up the phone, glance at your clock, turn on the lights, you are utilizing the talents of thousands. If you do not think so, try making your own phones, clocks or lightbulbs!

The people who happen to be at our jobs, churches or neighborhoods become our acquaintances simply

because they are there. And, of course, there is something quite commendable about showing love and
friendship toward whomever we meet. But we should
also be actively looking for talented people to help us
perfect the talents God has given us.

One of the first steps in learning and building a broad
repertoire is to find others in our talent area. As Oliver
Goldsmith noted, "People seldom improve when they
have no other model than themselves to copy." Those
who are on a higher level of expertise than we can teach
us many, many things. Those on our level can encourage and motivate us—and we them. And soon others
will start behind us, and we will have the privilege to
pass on the blessings and teachings we have received.

Gifted teachers are an invaluable blessing and always
worth seeking out. We must place high value on the
training they give us: "Hold on to instruction, do not let
it go; guard it well, for it is your life" (Proverbs 4:13).

Whatever talents you have, they can be improved on,
and this often involves people near you who also have
that talent. Do you want to learn to fly? Find a good
flight school and talk to others who have pilot's licenses.
Do you want to learn the bassoon? Find a good bassoon
instructor and a number of other bassoonists. Do you
want to learn to fish? Well, I am sure you have the idea.

Sometimes I am introduced as a self-taught musician,
meant as a compliment. It is true that, being born into
a loving but totally unmusical family and without any
music teachers before majoring in music at college, I
had to learn a good deal of music theory, history and
technique by myself. But there is certainly no aura about
the idea. Frankly, it would have been far better, quicker
and more efficient if I had had excellent teachers to
guide me and some music-loving colleagues to encourage me. And the same is true for you.

"Repertoire Maintenance"

In the preceding chapter we saw the importance of constantly improving our talents. In this chapter we have seen the need to build an ongoing repertoire within our talent areas. Now we will put the two concepts together, as we discuss "repertoire maintenance"—that is, improving on those things already in our repertoires.

Although I am a classical musician (a composer and conductor), I was once asked to speak at the Dove Awards ceremony held every year in Nashville. In the audience were many famous artists in the world of contemporary Christian music. They seemed appreciative of my topic, "The Biblical Concept of Excellence."

As I spoke many heads nodded their approval, but I was not sure I was really getting through. So I asked, "Has anyone here recently finished writing a new song?" Several hands went up, and I picked a young man to volunteer. (I learned his name later; you would probably know it.) He said he had completed a song the very day before. So I asked him what he would do now with this song.

"Tomorrow we are making a demo of it," he answered. "Next week we will record it for the market."

He announced this in a matter-of-fact voice, and no one there thought anything unusual about it—except me. I was incredulous. Classical composers generally take much longer about their compositions.

When he finally noticed my raised eyebrows, he ventured sheepishly, "Well, what would *you* do?"

I explained that after finishing a piece, I would probably take six months or so to polish it.

There was an audible gasp from the audience. Now *they* were incredulous. The young artist stammered, "My manager would never let me get away with that! The market just won't wait that long."

Unmoved, I asked him what he thought the result might be if he actually did spend six months polishing his song. He said, laughing, "If I did that, I could probably write the greatest song in the world!"

I waited until all the laughter subsided, then commented, "Don't you think it would be worth six months of your life to write the greatest song in the world?"

It became *very* quiet in that auditorium.

Perhaps I was a bit hard on this young songwriter, but I wanted to make an important point: We need to *polish* our work! In other words, when you finish something, you are not finished yet. Now is the polishing time, the period of improving what you have already created. Even a genius as masterful as Beethoven believed in this principle and considered it conceit if artists refused to polish their work. He said ruefully, "One must not hold one's self so divine as to be unwilling occasionally to make improvements in one's creations."

Nothing is so well made that it cannot be improved on. There is balance to be found; otherwise you might create only one thing and polish it for the rest of your life! But in our fast-paced world, the opposite is usually the case. We are often in a hurry to finish, and the polishing is left undone. Such polishing takes time, but it is always worth the extra effort.

Our Lord Jesus spent *three years* proclaiming the Gospel. Perhaps He could have finished in a few days, but instead He took the time needed for the task, to do it with excellence. Only at the end of three long years did He say to the Father, "I have brought you glory on earth by completing the work you gave me to do" (John 17:4). May we, as His followers, also be able to make this statement to the Father at the end of our lives.

Now that we have examined the need to improve ourselves and to build an ongoing repertoire, there is one more aspect of the broad topic of perfecting our talents:

preparedness. If you are ready to move on to the next step, read on!

To Consider and Discuss

1. Do you have long-range goals you are working toward? Middle-range goals? Short-range?

2. How can you relate practicing to your specific area of talent?

3. What books or other learning materials have you encountered in your talent field?

4. After working on something until you believe it is finished, how do you feel about further polishing it?

six

Preparedness

Make the most of every opportunity.

Colossians 4:5

One of the great beauties of the Bible, and surely one of the proofs of its inspired inerrancy, is the way God included innumerable aspects, all within the space of one book that you can hold in your hand. Many of His promises, prophecies and principles can be interpreted at a number of different levels and still be perfectly true. It is as if the Lord, in His wisdom and stewardship, crammed in many more messages to us than first meet the eye—almost like a new computer program that arrives compressed or "zipped" and can be unzipped to show all the information it actually contains.

An example of this is the verse that begins this chapter. We have all heard it used (correctly) to admonish Christians about personal evangelism—that is, we should make the most of every opportunity to share our faith. And indeed we should!

Yet making the most of every opportunity is a basic principle that should be incorporated into every area of our lives. In this passage Paul used personal evangelism *as an example* of the use of this principle. But other examples also apply.

For instance, when given a chance to serve our church, we should make the most of every opportunity. When we find ourselves with a family member who needs encouragement and is now open to counsel, we should make the most of every opportunity. And when we are faced with an unexpected prospect to use our God-given talent for God's glory, we should certainly make the most of every opportunity. We see that the same biblical principle has countless applications. As Samuel Johnson put it, "To improve the golden moment of opportunity, and catch the good that is within our reach, is the great art of life."

This principle, this making the most of every opportunity, is called *preparedness*.

Waiting Wistfully or Working *Toward?*

Some years ago I saw a rather dramatic example of the need for preparedness in the lives of talented Christians. Famed Christian opera singer Jerome Hines and I were working on a production at the Kennedy Center in Washington, D.C. The two of us were rehearsing in his studio about three in the afternoon when his secretary interrupted with an emergency phone call for him from New York.

The caller was the manager of the Metropolitan Opera Company, who had an urgent need. That very night the company was presenting an elaborate version of Verdi's opera *Don Carlo,* but the principal tenor had just been involved in a car accident. Furthermore, the two backup tenors were sick. The manager was frantic. Since opera singers learn many parts, whether they have performed them on stage or not, the manager was hoping that Hines knew of a new tenor he could solidly recommend to fill in the part that night.

While I waited and waited, Hines went through his address book with the manager. One by one possible substitutes were eliminated. Realizing that he had no concrete ideas to offer, Hines turned to me, quickly explained the desperate situation and asked if I might know of someone to recommend.

It was the moment I had been waiting for. Having heard one side of Hines' phone conversation, I already understood the problem. I had immediately thought of a friend, an excellent young opera singer whom I will call Norman. This Christian tenor was fabulous. He had been well trained in a world-class music school and had sung in several operas with major companies, yet he had never had an opportunity to sing at the Met, the pinnacle of opera in America. Norman even lived near New York City, and he had been praying for God to give him openings in his youthful career.

Waiting for my friend Norman to answer the hurried phone call, I thought, *This is it! Thank You, Lord, for allowing Norman this unbelievable opportunity.* Disraeli knew this principle well: "The secret to success in life is for a man to be ready for his opportunity when it comes."

My friend answered the phone, and I said, "Norman, this is Pat. I hope you're sitting down, because I have some fantastic news for you. Norman, you're going to be singing at the Met tonight!"

When a rather stunned voice replied, I hurriedly explained the circumstances, adding, "Praise God! Can you believe it! Verdi's *Don Carlo!* What a great tenor part!

And your voice is perfect for it. This could be the biggest break of your life!"

After further exclamations and congratulations, I finally heard a timorous voice say, "Uh, Pat, I don't know that role."

I was thunderstruck. "What do you mean, you don't know the role? It's *Don Carlo,* Verdi's *Don Carlo!* It's a great opera!"

"Of course it's a great opera. I know *of* the role. But I've never learned it myself. You see, I usually wait until an opera company calls and asks me to sing such and such a role. Then there is always time to go out and learn it. But I've never been asked to sing *Don Carlo* before, so I've never bothered to learn it."

By now you have guessed that, with great disappointment, my friend did not sing at the Met that night. That was ten years ago, and he has still not sung at the Met. God has used him in many other ways, of course. But he has never had such an incredible opportunity open to him again.

How true are the words of Mark Twain: "I was seldom able to see an opportunity until it had ceased to be one."

Avoiding the "If Only . . . "

A few months ago I told that story to a group of young opera singers. One of them remarked, "But one can't know all the operas out there," which is true. My point was not that every young tenor must know *Don Carlo,* but that each one should be learning new roles regularly, on his own, without anyone asking him.

Jerome Hines insists that a good opera singer should always learn two to three new roles each year, having them memorized and ready. When he was only twenty-six, he had already memorized twenty-six different opera roles and was adding more regularly. A few of them, he told me, he never was asked to sing, but he still kept them prepared. It will not surprise you, therefore, to find that Hines himself was hired to sing every year at the Met for more than four decades, more than any other singer in its history. That is a lot of operas!

We noted the practice of adding new roles in the previous chapter on building our repertoires. Now we need to discuss how to keep our repertoires fresh and ready to be used "in season and out of season" (2 Timothy 4:2). To use an analogy from a mechanic's world, it is one thing to build up a large and varied tool collection. It is quite another to keep the collection well-organized and maintained, so that you are always ready to pull out just the right tool as the occasion arises.

This might be called preventative maintenance. That is, we are trying to avoid a time in the future when we might have to utter the dreadful words, *If only. . . .* "If only I'd stayed in school!" "If only I'd worked harder!" "If only I hadn't quit that job!"

Obviously, part of our Christian walk is to try to make choices that do not bring these two doleful words to our minds or tongues. Proverbs 22:3 tells us, "A prudent man sees danger and takes refuge, but the simple keep going and suffer for it." I once spoke on this subject to the music department of a Christian college. The point must have been well taken, for a few days later I received a gift the students had made specially for me: a T-shirt with the words *If only . . .* printed on it but crossed out vigorously. This is a beloved trophy!

Can we actually be ready for everything at all times? Of course not. Even the minutemen in the Revolutionary War needed *a minute!* But they did not need an hour. They strove to be basically prepared all week, and then, when the bugle was blown, it only took a short time for the men to be completely ready. That is the picture we need in our minds. It is the same basic advice given by Ovid: "Let your hook always be cast. In the stream you least expect, there will be a fish."

Of course, there are some human limitations. Even the fastest sprinter cannot bound from his lunch table and run a four-minute mile. He needs preparation time. But those who are regularly "oiling and polishing" their repertoires need far less time for preparation than most of us.

You see, most people say that they long for a great opportunity. But remember this: A great opportunity will only make the unprepared look ridiculous. Can you do better at long-term preparation? Does such "oiling and polishing" of your work seem possible to you? How do you feel about the following words spoken by the great philosopher Francis Bacon? "If a man looks sharply and attentively, he shall see fortune, for though she be blind, she is not invisible."

How Big Is the Bottle Around You?

I once heard a fascinating story about a farmer who grew pumpkins, which grow in vines along the ground. Early in the season when his pumpkins were still tiny, the farmer was weeding the patch. At one point in his work among the vines, he noticed an empty liquor bottle that some careless passerby had thrown from a car window.

Picking up the old bottle, the farmer suddenly had a curious notion. Instead of placing the bottle in the trash, he set it near the vine and gingerly placed a tiny pumpkin inside, careful not to break the vine. Having initiated his little experiment, he left it on the ground and resumed his weeding.

What do you think the farmer found at harvesttime? After picking up dozens of large pumpkins and placing them in his truck bed, he spied the glass bottle. It was now filled with a runt pumpkin. The farmer broke the glass and saw that the little pumpkin had grown into the exact shape of the liquor bottle! It had grown as far as it could, but no farther.

A number of interesting things can be learned from this illustration, but I want to focus on just one. Having worked with hundreds of artists who have a variety of talents on many different talent levels, I have come to a certain conclusion: We are like the little pumpkin inside the bottle. We place arbitrary limits outside of us and say, "We can grow this far, but no farther."

Please note that I am not speaking of our actual talent levels (which are given by God), but of the *expectations* that we often put on them. It is as if we are saying to the Lord Himself, "I know that You've given me talents, and I'll do *this* with them—but don't ask me to do *that!*"

Thus, unlike the little pumpkin in the story, we are the ones who place these limiting bottles around us. Not the Lord, not fate, not our parents, not "the breaks"— *we* decide the size and shape of our own personal prisons. The famous Hollywood producer Samuel Goldwyn, who began as an impoverished immigrant, sums this up for us: "Everyone has bad breaks, but everyone also has opportunities. The man who can smile at the breaks and grab his chances gets on."

The good news is that we can change. We can, by God's grace (and often with a good deal of counseling, love and prayer), break out of our past constrictions. We need to remember 2 Timothy 1:7: "For God did not give us a spirit of timidity, but a spirit of power, of love and of self-discipline." It often takes time and determination, but such is the way the Lord has made us. So if you are one who feels that your talents were "held back" by such limitations, there is hope in Christ.

In other words, we need to recognize the difference between our talent levels and what might be called our "outside limitations." The former are given by God, the latter we give ourselves. As to our levels of talent . . . well, I do not know why God gives some more talent than others, just as I do not know why some pumpkins on the same vine grow larger than others. But I do know that we should try to improve upon our talents, as well as to break free from false limitations. These are *our* responsibilities.

That Wretched Spoiler: Nervousness

To illustrate how we can place limits around our abilities, let's take a classic problem: nervousness, often called stage fright or, more recently, performance anxiety.

I have seen gifted musicians come across as mediocre because they are too nervous to give a good performance. They are like the pumpkin, trying to grow and flourish normally, but running into an invisible wall. Sometimes these individuals are outshone by those with less natural talent but without such paralyzing nervousness. One might say that the latter are surrounded by a much larger bottle, with fewer limitations.

This syndrome is certainly not limited to those in the performing arts. It is everywhere, affecting thousands (believers as well as unbelievers) when they attempt to use their talents. It is the salesman about to meet a client, the place kicker trying to win the game with one field goal, the cook bringing out the Christmas feast, the student at the new school, the executive about to give a presentation to the board of directors, the pilot navigating his plane through a powerful storm.

Scripture is filled with portraits of nervousness and God's answers: To a trembling Moses at the burning bush, the Lord assures: "I will be with you" (Exodus 3:12). To Joshua, about to cross the Jordan at flood stage, He charges: "Be strong and courageous" (Joshua 1:6). To a timid Gideon, He asks: "Am *I* not sending you?" (Judges 6:14, emphasis added). To David and his out-numbered band of followers, He encourages: "I am going to give [them] into your hand" (1 Samuel 23:4). To Peter in the storm-tossed boat, Jesus reveals: "Take courage! It is I" (Matthew 14:27). To the disciples, about to lose their Master, Jesus consoles: "Do not let your hearts be troubled" (John 14:1). To the persecuted Paul, He offers strength: "Do not be afraid" (Acts 18:9).

What makes us nervous? The following two answers reveal much about ourselves and help us in our under-standing of this chapter's principal topic: preparedness.

In one of my earlier books (*Raising Musical Kids,* Servant, 1995), I wrote of a conversation I had with the great violinist and teacher James Buswell. He said that there are two fundamental reasons why performers get nervous. They are entirely independent of one another (though some of us may have both!) and need to be addressed as separate problems that have completely different solutions.

The two basic reasons we get nervous about sharing our talents are:

1. Insecurities/emotional impediments
2. A lack of preparedness

Regarding the first reason, people may dread walk-ing onto a stage or standing in front of a group to dis-play their talents because of any number of insecuri-ties—anything from painful childhood memories to irrational fears of rejection. Many professional performers around the world at this moment are with their psychiatrists or therapists, trying to find answers to this frustrating situation. Emotional barriers are a real and intense problem for even *very* talented people, especially those whose talents are in the public's eye.

In the performing arts world, the emotional side of this problem is dealt with constantly. Nevertheless my experiences have confirmed a need to spend more time on the second reason given above: preparedness. All too often performers are on the stage or in the spotlight when they are not at all prepared for such pressure. No wonder they are nervous!

Stacking the Odds in Your Favor

To explain this I will use a musical example, but this principle is applicable to all talent areas. Let's examine a young man practicing his trumpet. He has a difficult solo to perform next week with his ensemble (orchestra, band, whatever), and he is presently at work on this passage.

He plays it over and over, but seldom quite the same way twice. The passage improves gradually so that he plays it perfectly about one out of five attempts. He works even harder, until his accuracy approaches fifty percent. Every other time he plays this solo, it is perfect. Wonderful progress! At this point many young musicians will put their instruments away. They figure that they now have a pretty good chance to make it through the solo in the concert.

But, of course, this means that fifty percent of the time he will bomb. To perform now would be like playing Russian roulette with a pistol of only two chambers! Furthermore, since the heightened emotion of playing for an audience is far stronger than that of being alone in a practice room, which of the one-out-of-two odds is really more likely to happen? Right. This young man is *nowhere* near ready for a performance. He needs to go back to the practice room.

Here is what should have happened in his preparation. Once he had practiced enough to play the passage correctly every other time, he should have continued. He should bring this up to playing it correctly two out of three times. Then three out of four, and higher. Many world-class performers would not dream of walking onto a stage until they know that they can play the music perfectly ninety-nine out of one hundred times. They become those whom Virgil described: "They can because they think they can."

Is ultra-development difficult? Of course it is. You become like the silver in Psalm 12, "refined in a furnace of clay, purified seven times" (Psalm 12:6). This is the price of excellent preparedness.

Let's face it. No matter how insecure or emotionally stricken you might be, if you absolutely *knew* that you could perform perfectly ninety-nine out of one hundred times, then you would be much less nervous walking into the spotlight. After all, the odds are stacked so highly in your favor.

Preparedness is the best way to deal with this greatest limiting factor, nervousness.

"But Didn't Jesus Say . . . ?"

Is it not true, you might ask, that Jesus said *not* to prepare, at least in one instance?

This refers to the passage in Matthew 10, where He describes the persecution the faithful will endure. Our Lord says, "But when they arrest you, do not worry about what to say or how to say it. At that time you will be given what to say, for it will not be you speaking, but the Spirit of your Father speaking through you" (verses 19–20). What does such an instruction say to all this talk of preparedness?

First of all, three key words in this verse are *At that time*. The Lord gave some instructions that were for all times and others that were *time specific*. It seems that the instructions of Matthew 10 are meant to be used in specific times, notably when being persecuted and on trial for our faith.

Second of all, note that Jesus did not say, "Do not be prepared." He said, "Do not *worry*." This is a critical distinction. And we have already seen that one of the best ways to avoid the trap of worry and nervousness is to be well prepared. The Scriptures are replete with examples of good preparation that we are to emulate: Joseph planning for the coming famine, David preparing for the Temple to be built, the disciples preparing for the Passover meal. Recall that in 1 Peter 3:15 we are commanded: "*Always be prepared* to give an answer to everyone who asks you to give the reason for the hope that you have" (emphasis added).

Our job is to refrain from worry but not from the work of preparation. Indeed, hard work is often an excellent way to keep us from the snare of worry. Consider Thomas Edison's lighthearted—but ultimately valid—words: "As a cure for worrying, work is better than whiskey."

Matthew 25 gives us further direction on the subject of preparedness, in Jesus' Parable of the Ten Virgins. As you recall, five virgins were foolish (unprepared for the unexpected) and five were wise (bringing extra oil for their lamps). The wise virgins were commended and rewarded, but the foolish ones were left out of the wedding feast. At the end of the parable, Jesus gave a summary of the lesson in three words:

"Therefore keep watch." He could have said, "Therefore always be prepared."

It is by misunderstanding this principle that many Christians grow confused about the concept of "living by faith." They fail to see that God works through such natural means as preparation. Perhaps the five foolish virgins were "living by faith" and trusting in the Lord to replenish their oil supply miraculously! And, of course, God certainly had the power to do so. But He expects us to live up to the responsibilities He has given us. And one of them is to be prepared for the opportunities that He sends into our lives.

We Prepare by the Manner in Which We Use Our Time

By now I trust that you are convinced of the importance of preparedness, especially in regard to the talents we possess. Here comes the practical side: looking at how we go about this, how we find a way to incorporate preparedness as a lifestyle—whatever our gifting happens to be.

All of this has to do with the manner in which we use our time, that is, the choices we make regarding the time we have. The five foolish virgins had the same 24-hour day before the wedding feast as the five wise ones. As C. S. Lewis reminds us, "The future is something that everyone reaches at the rate of sixty minutes an hour, whatever he does, wherever he is." It is in the way that the wise virgins *used* their time in deliberate preparation that led to their eventual reward.

This rather obvious fact is often overlooked. You will hear it said that someone is successful because he "had the breaks" or "had fewer obstacles" or "had more money" or whatever. This is an illusion. Those who are successful are usually the people who made the wisest choices in life and used the time they had in the wisest manner. Again, it comes back to the use of our time.

To begin with, let's divide your waking hours into two types of time. In the first category, we include the dozens of things that simply have to be done: work, related travel, sleeping, eating and so on. You have little choice but to do these things, so we will call this compulsory time. This is a large part of your average day.

Now, there is also time (sometimes in small slices) in which you have more control. You may read a book, watch TV, practice within your talent area, call a friend or do a thousand other things that you choose freely to do. With your busy lifestyle, you may imagine that this is a rather small part of your day, yet it would probably surprise you to find how much of your time is actually in this category. We will call this elective time.

Take a moment to divide your day into these two categories. Compulsory time is fairly easy to figure out. You simply have to do those things whether you want to or not. This is the work you do, as the Scripture says, "by the sweat of your brow" (Genesis 3:19).

But how you spend your elective time needs to be considered carefully.

Your elective time, whether a moment or an hour, might be divided into two categories: (1) activities that relax and entertain you for the moment and (2) activities that move you toward a goal in the future. Of the two, most of us might lean toward relaxation and entertainment. This is something each of us needs and we should not feel guilty about it. But should we spend *all* of our elective time in short-term activities?

Suppose you set aside some of your elective time every day to work on preparing for a future goal in your talent area. This does not mean that you should eliminate all forms of relaxing activity. It means that at the end of each day, you should be able to look over the previous hours and find some activity you chose to do with long-term consequences.

Using even a few moments each day in this manner has such a powerful cumulative effect that it can utterly revolutionize your life. Barbara Bush, wife of one president and mother of another, understands this day-by-day principle: "You don't just luck into things. You build step by step, whether it's friendships or opportunities." Using even a little of your elective time each day to prepare for the future will equip you for the opportunities that the Lord will bring about in His time and help you follow Jesus' loving injunction not to worry.

The Time Gauge

God has given us many talents. How well we utilize these talents for Him depends primarily on the choices we make about our time. Let's go to a higher level of stewardship, therefore, and find a consistent way to use the time we have to maximize our talents.

I give below a recommended exercise that will mean an investment of a few hours, but it will provide a daily tool that can help you for years to come.

Most of us are kept so busy that we seldom reflect on the direction of our lives. In any given year, we are involved in a variety of activities; we would like to minimize some and spend more time on others. What we need is a "time gauge," so that we can look at a day, week or month and note, "I should spend more time in such and such" or "I spent too much time doing this or that."

Here is a four-step process for creating a time gauge for your own life (pray for guidance throughout this exercise):

Step 1

Write down a list of all the different categories that represent your present life. These are broad areas that might include: your home life, your work life (or school life), your relationships (parents, wife, husband, children, friends), your church life, your talent area(s), your personal time (reading, for example), your hobbies/interests and your devotional life (between you and the Lord). This will, of course, be different for every person and may involve more or fewer categories.

Add to this list any categories that you believe should be a part of your life but are not currently. (No priorities are necessary yet.) When finished, go to the next step.

Step 2

Take the categories in your first list and break them down into the various activities associated with them.

For example, if you had "devotional time" in the first list, you might write something like "Bible study, prayer, memorizing Bible verses" beside it. Do this for each of your original categories and you will soon come up with a list of activities that roughly describe your present life. (Again, no priorities are necessary yet; just write down every activity that relates to the categories you have listed.)

Be sure that you have added any categories and related activities to this list that you believe *should* be a part of your life. When finished, go to the next step.

Step 3

Now take the second list (all of your activities from Step 2) and carefully prioritize each item.

Ouch! This is painfully difficult and sometimes rather subjective, but do it anyway. Place a *1* beside the activity that you believe is the most important (or should be the most important) of your life. Place a *2* beside the activity that is next in importance and so on until your entire list is prioritized numerically. This could be a hard task, but it is a necessary one. Think like Napoleon: "Nothing is more difficult, and therefore more precious, than to be able to decide." Do not stop until you have decided numerical priorities for each of your activities.

Step 4

And now the final touch. You have before you a list of prioritized activities that should reflect either your present life or the life toward which you are striving. The preceding is always a beneficial exercise, causing you to consider the activities of your life and their various degrees of importance. Many time management courses stop here and leave you to contemplate your lists. But a final step will create a "time gauge" to measure how closely your daily activities really come to your ideals. Without such a gauge to measure by, we will be unprepared to "make the most of every opportunity" (Colossians 4:5).

Recopy your prioritized-activities list so that number one is at the top, then number two below it and so on, all the way down to the last item. Now carefully divide this list into the following six categories:

D.D.   Definitely Daily (I will *definitely* do this *every day*)

P.D.   Possibly Daily (I will *try* to do this *every day*)

D.W.   Definitely Weekly (I will *definitely* do this *every week*)

P.W.   Possibly Weekly (I will *try* to do this *every week*)

D.M.   Definitely Monthly (I will *definitely* do this *every month*)

P.M.   Possibly Monthly (I will *try* to do this *every month*)

Be prayerful and take your time with this. Remember that this is entirely between you and the Lord. Your list need not be shown to anyone else. Be utterly realistic. Do not promise to make regular commitments that are impractical. You should particularly avoid placing too many activities in the higher categories.

Perhaps I should give a personal example, especially concerning this last point. On my first list, I have seven broad areas of life, and on my second list I have written twenty-five activities that reflect my life at the moment. My number-one priority is related neither to my family nor to my ministry; it is my quiet time alone with God. And this is the only activity that I placed in the "Definitely Daily" category.

You may think poorly of me that I do not place my family in this D.D. category. (My activities as a husband and a father are in the second category, which I try to do daily if at all possible.) The reason is simple: I may be out of town, away from my family, perhaps even unable to contact them. But there is never a day when I cannot have contact with the Lord. Christ told us that to love God is "the first and greatest commandment" (Matthew 22:38). That sounds like top priority to me! For an activity to be in the D.D. category, it must be done every day without exception.

Once you have finished this final step, take your completed list and place it where you can see it every day. Look at it each morning, praying that God will help you to walk out those priorities during the day. Then look at it again at night before going to sleep. How did your day compare with the list? Furthermore, make a special reading of it weekly and monthly to check whether or not you are actually living the priorities you have made.

Obviously this is a long-term matter, and it will be altered over the years. Some of the activities on my list have changed, as different seasons in life produce different priorities. But it gives me a gauge, a plumb line, for regular examination of how closely my ideals are meeting with my actual day-to-day life.

Putting It All Together: Trust

The first three chapters of this book discussed the different ways in which to discover the talents that God has given us. The middle three have dealt with the necessary honing and perfecting of this talent, whether it be great or small. Before going on to the final three chapters, concerned with actually using one's talents, let's take stock of our situation.

It may be safely assumed that you, the reader, are presently aware of at least some of the talents within you. (If not, reread the first three chapters!) I hope that these middle three chapters have made enough of an impression that you realize the need to work on your talents before using them publicly.

Before moving to the three chapters of the last section, consider further this aspect of timing. You may have read these middle chapters about preparation in a few hours or a few weeks. Yet the time of preparation is not over. Indeed, for most of us, this will take many years. Ultimately the task of perfecting one's talents is the work of a lifetime. Einstein once commented on his own intellectual talents: "I think and think for months, for years. Ninety-nine times the conclusion is false. The one hundredth time I am right." But each of the first ninety-nine times was an improvement on its predecessor, attempts that led him closer to the right answer.

In other words, as you read on and learn principles for using your talents, do not be hasty about moving forward to use them. Remember what we have learned about preparation and God's timing.

When we first read the story of David to our young boys, they were struck with the time gap between his anointing by Samuel (in 1 Samuel 16) and his actual assumption of the kingship (in 2 Samuel 5). There are some twenty chapters—even more years—of preparation. We have already seen that David used that time to "build his repertoire" of experiences. But did he really need that many years to prepare? Could God not have brought David to the kingship earlier?

Perhaps God could have, but He did not. We do not know why the Lord sometimes waits years before opening a door for us. We do not know why some seemingly undeserving people are blessed with great talent while many devout saints are somewhat "underblessed" in this area. We do not know why some person's talent goes unrecognized while another is acclaimed internationally. To use our talents for Christ we need to *know* very little, but we need to trust very much.

And we must have patience to wait for the Lord's time. George MacDonald wrote that "the principal part of faith is patience," and Michelangelo said that "genius is eternal patience." That kind of genius we all need.

We must trust that God has a reason for giving us talents, whether we or anyone else sees this reason or not. We must trust that God has His time for their fruition and His purposes in withholding this fruition long after we feel ready. And we must see these talents as ultimately between ourselves and the Lord—to be given freely back to Him.

Before moving into the final section of this book, consider these words of Abraham Lincoln: "Without the assistance of the Divine Being, I cannot succeed. With that assistance, I cannot fail." This is somewhat of a scriptural paraphrase, since "apart from [Jesus, I] can do nothing" (John 15:5), but "I can do everything through [Jesus] who gives me strength" (Philippians 4:13).

It is with such trust in God that we now dare to use our talents for His glory.

To Consider and Discuss

1. Remember the illustration about the farmer and the pumpkin in the glass bottle. How can you relate this to the expectations you have about yourself?

2. Do you become nervous easily? What have you done that has helped?

3. How much of your daily time could be considered compulsory? How much is elective?

4. Applying the time gauge to your life, what are your highest categories? How are they reflected in your daily schedule?

Part 3

Using
Your Talents

seven

Using Your Talents at Home

She sets about her work vigorously; her arms are strong for her tasks.

Proverbs 31:17

Jesus gave some important last-minute instructions to His disciples before He ascended into heaven: "You will be my witnesses in Jerusalem, and in all Judea and Samaria, and to the ends of the earth" (Acts 1:8). With these words, the Lord gave them a plan of action that would begin right where they were and spread gradually outward. It demonstrated a principle that can also be applied to our talents.

Discovering that God has given us talents can be so exciting we dream of playing at Carnegie Hall this week! Or at least at church. Yet these are not the places we should start. Before we go "to the ends of the earth," we should look for ways to express our talents right where we are: at home.

The modern world has inflicted terrible damage on the image and dignity of the home. The traditional family unit is under attack from a number of different enemies. Women, in particular, have been told that they are wasting their talents if they elect to stay home with their children. Many in our culture have become so career-minded that the home is nothing more than a place to sleep at night: All that is "important" takes place elsewhere.

This is a grossly unbiblical picture of this paramount institution that the Lord created from the very beginning. Jesus spent much of His ministry teaching in homes. The earliest churches all met in homes. This was not because of a lack of building space or because of persecution: It was God's original design.

Our lives should revolve around our homes, not our jobs and not even our churches. Whenever this gets reversed, we are out of line and unbalanced. The home is where our most important relationships come together. And it is also a primary place for the exercise of our talents.

In the final three chapters of this book, we will examine a number of important principles (including examples of famous individuals who exemplify each) about our God-given talents. This chapter highlights twelve principles concerning the use of our talents—whatever they may be—in our homes.

Principle No. 1: Use Your Talents to Minister to Your Children

Millions of people are familiar with *The Hobbit* and *The Lord of the Rings,* but probably few know of their origin. These books brought a vast amount of fame to

John Ronald Reuel Tolkien (1892–1973), all of which was quite a surprise to him. A professor of Anglo-Saxon literature at Oxford, he scribbled the opening sentence of the first book, "In a hole in the ground there lived a hobbit," while correcting examination papers.

Tolkien later expanded the story for the purpose of telling entertaining tales to his young children. Even after *The Hobbit* was successfully published and his publisher asked for a sequel, Tolkien was still writing for his family. Chapter after chapter of *The Lord of the Rings* was mailed to his son, Christopher, a pilot for the Royal Air Force—who later became his father's principal editor.

Sad to say, many children growing up today have little idea of their parents' talents, because these talents are never used on their behalf. This sharing of ourselves is part of the provision we are to give to our children, as Scripture dictates: "Children should not have to save up for their parents, but parents for their children" (2 Corinthians 12:14). A parent's talents not only enhance the quality of life in the home but also serve as excellent modeling for the children to emulate.

What could you create for your family? You may not be able to write books like Tolkien, but you possess talents that should be given to your children as much as to your peers. Ask yourself *What can I do creatively to bless my family?* (And yes, I have written a novel just for my children!)

Principle No. 2: Use Your Talent to Nurture Talent in Others

Every organization needs organization! Every time you hop on a plane, go out to eat, buy a car or watch a TV program, you are able to do so because someone (maybe many "someones") has performed a great deal of organizing. Every company in the world is looking for good organizers, and yet people often do not realize that this is a talent as much as playing the piano is a talent. And perhaps the best place to demonstrate organizational talent is in the home.

Millions of people have been affected by the ministry of John and Charles Wesley, founders of the Methodist Church. But their primary influence was that of a godly mother who was an organizer *par excellence*. Susanna Wesley (1669–1742) was born the twenty-fifth child of her family, so she must have seen the need for good organization at an early age. She grew in this talent as she matured and brought her gifts to fulfillment in her marriage and the family she raised.

The wife of Samuel Wesley, an Anglican minister, she bore nineteen children (ten survived). Her husband was away often on church business, and the household administration was squarely on Susanna's shoulders. All but one of the children learned to read by the age of five. Her children were taught to play quietly, to eat what was placed before them and to confess their faults.

This amazing woman (who would surely be giving seminars today!) made it a rule for herself to spend an hour alone with each child over the period of a week. This took a talent for home organization that directly influenced the church organization seen later in her sons. One can easily imagine Susanna teaching her children God's laws: "Impress them on your children. Talk about them when you sit at home and when you walk along the road, when you lie down and when you get up" (Deuteronomy 6:7).

The result of using her talent to nurture others is seen in the fruit of her children—who led tens of thousands to Christ. Certainly most of these converts never met Susanna Wesley. Yet without the faithful use of her unsung talent, it is doubtful that John and Charles Wesley would have shared her organizational skill and disciplined life, or moved on to such prolific ministries. Her talents were not displayed in the public eye; rather they created an atmosphere for nurturing similar talents in those under her care.

Principle No. 3: Encourage Your Children's Own Talents

Everyone knows of the great composer Wolfgang Amadeus Mozart. But what about Leopold Mozart, his father? The elder Mozart (1719–1787) was also a composer, though not a very good one. Nevertheless, without his ongoing encouragement, his son might never have come to such prominence. For this father recognized his son's talent at an early age, found him the best teachers, arranged for concerts, traveled with him and made certain that Mozart's talents reached fruition.

One of the primary duties of a Christian parent is to help his or her children discover their talents and encourage their growth. This means that we assist them in trying a number of talent areas, applauding their efforts and successes, and arranging for excellent instruction. Parents should be the ultimate *encouragers,* as alluded to in 1 Thessalonians 2:11–12: "For you know that we dealt with each one of you as a father deals with his own children, encouraging, comforting and urging you to live lives worthy of God." Whether we are encouraging them in the Christian walk or in developing their talents, encouragement is one of the greatest investments we can make in our children's future.

Most of the time when this subject is discussed, people think of piano lessons or soccer teams. Music and athletics can be important parts of one's education, but these are only two possibilities. As we have seen in previous chapters, there are *many* different types of talent— and each needs to be encouraged in our children.

Parents need to think "out of the box." Since my wife and I are both musicians, we arranged to have our children take music lessons on various instruments. But for one of our sons, it soon became clear that music was not his thing. He had a strong aptitude for science and philosophy, subjects in which neither of his parents possessed any expertise. So we found a skilled scientist in our church and arranged for weekly "lessons." They met for several years, and this man has had a profound influence on my son's life.

Does your child have mechanical talents? How about organizational or communication talents? These should be encouraged and honed. This may mean, of course, a bit of extra work on your part (as I write this, I am waiting for one of my sons to finish rehearsal for a play in which he is acting), but it will be worth it to see your children flourish.

Principle No. 4: Listen to Your Family's Ideas

Too many of us tend to compartmentalize our lives, leaving behind our thoughts of family when we drive off to work. Yet God often uses members of our families to bring us excellent ideas for the workplace—*if* we will listen to them and not just rely on the "experts." A good example of this is seen in the life of Walt Disney (1901–1966).

When Disney set up his small studio in Hollywood, one of his first successes was a fully synchronized sound cartoon entitled *Steamboat Willie*. It featured a mouse that Disney had given the tongue-tying name "Mortimer Mouse." Fortunately he listened to his wife's suggestion to replace the name *Mortimer* with her melodious-sounding idea, *Mickey* Mouse.

Another idea from his family life gave Disney one of his greatest projects. He and his wife often took their children to amusement parks, and they sat and watched while the children played on various kiddie rides. Dad and Mom Disney talked about the need for a park where the entire family could have fun together. Such conversations eventually led to the 1957 opening of Disneyland, the most successful amusement park in history with 6.7 million people visiting in its first ten years.

When you hear your spouse's or children's ideas, do you ignore them? Or do you realize that the Lord may be speaking to you through those closest to you? If "from the lips of children and infants" (Psalm 8:2) our God accepts praise, then surely He can give those same family members creative ideas that we would be foolish to overlook.

Principle No. 5: Use Your Skills to Enable Others to Minister

When we think about someone with great medical skill, we usually consider a doctor in a medical environment. Yet Katie Luther (1499–1552) was ahead of her time, and most of her work was for one patient, her husband, the great reformer Martin Luther. When he married the former nun, they scarcely knew each other, but her skills enabled Luther to achieve far more than he could have without her.

After many years of persecution, Luther's body was frail. He had frequent bouts of illness for which the crude doctoring of his day could do little. Yet the nursing talents of his wife, Katie, brought him back to health again and again. Luther called his wife "the morning star of Wittenberg," admiring the way she rose at four A.M. each day to care for her many responsibilities. Although she left no writings of her own, many of the important documents written by her husband would never have been penned without her skill and care.

Likewise, our examples of service can have an impact far beyond anything our eyes can see. When my mother was quite young, she contracted a dangerous disease. To help combat this illness, her parents hired a full-time nurse, who stayed by my mother's side day and night. After many weeks the illness finally passed. The young patient was so impressed by the talents of this nurse that she resolved to become a nurse herself. Years later my mother was graduated from nursing school and began her career, in which she eventually became head nurse for a major hospital. All from a caring example of skillful ministry.

We should never forget the power of ministering *to one person*. Some of us may be called to reach the masses, but many of us are simply required to use our talents faithfully for one person, so that he or she may be released for ministry. Paul wanted the entire world to know Christ, but he spent a great deal of time with his friend Timothy. This training enabled the younger man to bring the Gospel to places Paul never visited. Paul declared of Timothy, "I have no one else like him, who takes a genuine interest in your welfare" (Philippians 2:20). Sometimes we use our talents to minister, while at other times we use our talents to enable the ministry of others. In either case God is glorified!

Principle No. 6: Bring Together Your Family Talent

The Von Trapp Family Singers were immortalized in the 1965 movie *The Sound of Music*. The actual family included a number of fine singers, and they performed together to great acclaim. Few of us come from such an overtly talented family, but undoubtedly every family has some area of talent in common.

In a world where the institution of the family is under attack, such a talent bond can become a tremendous testimony. Consider the ministry of a contemporary musical duo called "Aaron Jeffrey"—performers Jeffrey Benward and his son Aaron. Their recordings are fantastic, and their testimony has a powerful impact.

Aaron states, "Our goal is to show a positive parent/child relationship and to be role models for fathers and their sons, or parents and their children. Every social problem that we have today can be traced back to a dysfunctional family life. We want to address these problems, not only by our songs but by simply being who we are." By their wonderful example, they display the biblical standard for the family, as given in 1 Timothy 3:4 (in a passage about spiritual leadership): "He must manage his own family well and see that his children obey him with proper respect."

We cannot all be great singers, of course. If my son and I got up to sing for an audience, we would quickly clear the room! But are there other areas of talent shared by your family? This could include athletics, mechanical or organizational projects, community hospitality, or any number of other possibilities. Not only will you be a blessing to others, but this could become a strong bond between each member of your family.

Principle No. 7: Use Your Talents to Bring Your Family to Christ

As we have seen from previous chapters, many of our talents are inherited from our parents. The preaching and writings of the great Augustine (354–430) sprang from a tremendous gift for communication, which he used to communicate the truths of the Christian faith.

This talent was both inherited from and inspired by his mother, Monica (333–387).

Born into a moderately wealthy family, Monica had been led to Christ by an old maidservant. Forced to marry an unbeliever named Patricius, she began a faithful and loving campaign to communicate the Gospel to her husband and children. This was not with incessant nagging but as Scripture advises: "They may be won over without words by the behavior of their wives, when they see the purity and reverence of your lives" (1 Peter 3:1–2).

Because of her skill as a peacemaker, Monica was often called to settle disputes in the community. She always communicated the simple truth, so people knew exactly where they were with Monica. When her son, Augustine, began to live an immoral lifestyle, she admonished him carefully with the truth but without the harshness that might have broken their relationship. This skillful use of her talents was rewarded in full: both her husband and her son became Christians, and Augustine's writings have had tremendous impact on the Church for many centuries.

Too often we equate communication skills with a person who talks a great deal. But words are only one means of communication. Those who are truly gifted in this area look at the whole picture: words, looks, feelings, timing and many other factors of good communication. Not only can the effective use of such a talent bring one's family to Christ, it also can have an impact on the lives of thousands.

Principle No. 8: Find Inspiration for Talent from the Beauty of Your Family

History is replete with stories of talented people who were inspired by members of their own families. One of these was the renowned seventeenth-century Dutch painter we know as Rembrandt (1606–1669). The son of a poor miller, this young man moved to Amsterdam where he began to eke out a living painting portraits. It was difficult at first; in 1631 he painted only one commissioned portrait.

Then Rembrandt van Rijn met Saskia van Uylenburgh, fell deeply in love and was suddenly *very* motivated to succeed. His opportunity came when the Surgeons' Guild of Amsterdam commissioned a work for its clubhouse. His *Anatomy Lesson* showed such genius that Rembrandt became famous instantly. Within a year he had painted sixteen portraits and raised his price to five hundred guilders apiece—a sum paid only to masters.

Having finally impressed Saskia's parents, the young painter was allowed to marry her and his creativity increased even more. He was a true example of the proverb "He who finds a wife finds what is good and receives favor from the LORD" (Proverbs 18:22). Although he was now sought by the nobility of Europe, Rembrandt's favorite subject to paint was always his wife. He painted her portraits over and over again and used her as the model in dozens of other works. If you compare the women in Rembrandt's magnificent biblical paintings, you will notice that many of them are modeled from the face of his beloved wife.

There have been dozens of other artists throughout history whose principal inspiration came from within their families. Consider the many artist couples, such as the poets Robert and Elizabeth Barrett Browning or the musicians Clara and Robert Schumann. Not all of us share our talent fields with members of our families, but we can all find creative inspiration right in our own homes.

Principle No. 9: Seek Counsel from Family Members Whose Talents Give Insight

The Scriptures admonish us that "plans fail for lack of counsel, but with many advisers they succeed" (Proverbs 15:22). Obviously, when we have decisions to make, we need to seek good counsel from those whose gifts also lie in our talent areas. If this counsel is also within our own families, there is all the more reason to seek it out. A perfect example is found in the lives of husband and wife team Pierre Curie (1859–1906) and Marie Curie (1867–1934), the discoverers of radium.

The scientific progress made by this heroic and talented couple took many years of relentless labor. Much of the laboratory work put them both in close contact with dangerous radioactive materials. Furthermore, they were raising a family, teaching and living on a limited income. Yet their efforts were rewarded with success, and in 1898 they announced jointly the discovery of two new elements, polonium and radium.

Soon after the second discovery, it was found that radium could be used in the war against cancer. Engineers from America wanted to use radium in this way, yet they could not produce it without the secret of the Curies' delicate experiments. They wrote Pierre Curie for information, and he immediately went to his wife to discuss the situation.

After summarizing the letter from America, Pierre told her, "We have two choices. We can describe the results of our research without reserve, including the processes of purification." Marie gave a gesture of approval and answered, "Yes, naturally." Her husband continued, "Or else, we can consider ourselves to be the 'inventors' of radium, patent the technique of treating pitchblende, and assure ourselves of rights over the manufacture of radium throughout the world." In effect,

Pierre was explaining that the choice was between continuing in poverty or claiming riches.

Marie reflected a moment, then answered, "It is impossible. It would be contrary to the scientific spirit." Her husband smiled and said, "I shall write tonight, then, to the American engineers, and give them the information they ask for." In so doing, they gave their great discoveries to the world and thus enabled thousands to benefit from their talents.

When we have major decisions to make, our first imperative is prayer. Then we should seek counsel of those whose talents and experiences give them insight into the situation. But we should never omit those in our own families, whom God often uses to give us direction. Sometimes the very answer you seek will come from young voices around the dinner table.

Principle No. 10: Display Your Workplace Talents Before Your Family

Granted, it is often difficult and impractical to minister some of our workplace talents directly to our family. A brain surgeon cannot exactly operate on his children every night! Nevertheless, there are ways to demonstrate our talent areas before our families with excellent results. For many, this may mean taking your children to your jobs occasionally. Others may be able to bring your jobs home.

Antonin Dvořák (1841–1904), composer of the *New World Symphony* and many other masterpieces, was a true "family man." Unlike some composers who worked in solitude, Dvořák wrote much of his finest work at the kitchen table—surrounded by his noisy children and his wife baking bread. Though he became a famous musician, his work could always be interrupted by his youngest child.

An amusing picture of the Dvorák household was recorded by one of his music students: "His children were permitted to invade his studio at all times, even when the composer was at serious work. My daily lessons were usually taken with the accompaniment of grimacing boys and girls hidden behind articles of furniture or appearing at unexpected moments in doorways out of their father's sight."

When I first had an office in our home, I was often frustrated to find Play-Doh on the computer keyboard or LEGO pieces in the filing cabinets. Sometimes I talked to a famous musician on the phone while babies cried in the background. But when our ministry grew and moved into a professional office, I missed the family atmosphere. Later we solved the problem by erecting a separate building next to our home, which houses our ministry's headquarters. Now when my children come home from school, they drop in the office and I can take a break and see them.

Not everyone has an option like mine, but kids do love to see Dad and Mom "at work." Always remember the Scripture, "Parents are the pride of their children" (Proverbs 17:6). Try to find a way to bring this principle into your family life.

Principle No. 11: Realize That Your Talent May Be Known Only to You, Your Family and God

On December 10, 1830, one of the world's greatest poets was born in Amherst, Massachusetts. Today the works of Emily Dickinson (1830–1886) are loved by millions and studied by every literature student. Yet during her lifetime she spent almost every day in her home with her family, writing poems that few were allowed to see.

As a poet Emily Dickinson was virtually unknown. Only through strong encouragement was she persuaded to have a few of her poems published. Dozens of her other masterpieces were found among her papers after her death.

Reading her poetry, two aspects of her inner life are consistently present. One is her deeply robust—if somewhat unconventional—relationship to God. It shines through much of her work, such as in this short poem:

> I never saw a moor,
> I never saw the sea;
> Yet know I how the heather looks,
> And what a wave must be.
>
> I never spoke with God,
> Nor visited in Heaven;
> Yet certain am I of the spot
> As if the chart were given.

The second aspect of this poet's life is a remarkable lack of desire for fame and recognition by the world, as depicted in one of her most popular poems:

> I'm Nobody! Who are you?
> Are you—Nobody—too?
> Then there's a pair of us!
> Don't tell! they'd advertise—you know!
>
> How dreary—to be—Somebody!
> How public—like a Frog—
> To tell one's name—the lifelong June—
> To an admiring Bog!

In our day, when people often crave the world's attention, hiring publicists to get their names into the papers, it is refreshing to find one who knew better. Whatever motivated Emily Dickinson to create her brilliant work, it was never the desire for man's recognition. She certainly realized that she had a talent from God. But she took seriously the biblical admonition "Do not claim a place among great men" (Proverbs 25:6). She chose to be content using it within the walls of her own home.

Principle No. 12—Always Place Your Family Above Your Talents

This last principle is not illustrated by a famous person, but I cannot help but relay this episode. In the first chapter I mentioned that my father, Ed Kavanaugh (1917–1999), was a mailman, then a postal supervisor. Being talented at working with people, he received a number of promotions and was soon one of the top managers in his area.

His talent and hard work were bringing him great rewards, but at the height of his career, family matters began to cloud his life. Specifically, my older brother started to move in "the wrong crowd," and Dad saw that he needed to spend far more time with his family. To the astonishment of his colleagues, Dad abandoned his career climb and took a semi-retirement position (managing a neighborhood post office) so he could be available for my brother's needs. You may be sure that God honored my father's sacrifice.

This is a book about talents. But we should always keep them within a set of biblical priorities, which means "family first." Suppose your talents were successfully recognized and applauded by everyone—could you then abandon them if necessary for the sake of your family? This is a difficult area for many of us. Even though God has given us talents, we must never forget the verse that says, "Nobody should seek his own good, but the good of others" (1 Corinthians 10:24). There may be times in our lives when it will be imperative to make such a sacrifice, and we should prepare our hearts for such a contingency.

Like so many aspects of the Christian walk, using our talents is ultimately between us and God. There are times when our gifts may be openly praised, and there are times when we must "lay them on the altar" and wait. Furthermore, there are times when the Lord would have us use our talents for the edification of His Church—which brings us to our next chapter.

To Consider and Discuss

1. What are some of the ways you can encourage the talents of those in your family?

2. How would you rate yourself at listening to the ideas and opinions of your family members?

3. Is there someone in your family (or extended family) who is not a believer? How can you use your gifts to encourage him or her toward faith in Christ?

4. How difficult would it be for you to lay down your talents for the sake of your family?

eight

Using Your Talents in the Church

To prepare God's people for works of service, so that the body of Christ may be built up. . . .

Ephesians 4:12

The church is more than a building where Christians meet with one another. It is a gathering of the Body of Christ, communion with the saints—those of our own day, plus the heritage of those who have gone before us. It should be a major part of our lives, second only to the home itself. Furthermore, the church should be a primary place where we take our God-given talents and offer them back to the Lord.

Unfortunately, this does not often occur. Pastors everywhere speak of the "80–20 rule"—that is, eighty percent of the work in the church is done by twenty percent of the people. These faithful twenty percent are indeed blessed and use their lives and talents to bless others. But the remaining eighty percent are apparently leaving their talents at the church door.

This does not mean, of course, that eighty percent of all Christians fail to use their talents entirely. They are (we would hope) using them in the home or in the workplace. Nevertheless, all of us should strive to take our gifts into the church—not simply our bodies and our tithes. No one is exempt from the admonishment of Galatians 6:10: "Therefore, as we have opportunity, let us do good to all people, *especially to those who belong to the family of believers*" (emphasis added).

I work primarily with musicians, and it always startles me to find that many professional Christian musicians play for dozens of different occasions and venues, but seldom (or never) for their own local churches! Doubtless this problem is not limited to musicians. How many churches have congregations with gifted businessmen, artists, writers and a hundred other talents that remain unused in the church?

Someone may argue, truthfully enough, that their talents have been painfully unappreciated within their churches. Others may contend that their church's policy of allowing anyone to participate creates a wide range of talent and lack-of-talent that is difficult to mix. Still others will point out (as I mentioned in an earlier chapter) that the "forgiving" attitude of the church has encouraged a good deal of mediocrity.

All these objections are true. One could probably find a hundred reasonable objections to using one's talents for the church. But Galatians 6:10 still remains. We need to put our excuses aside and determine to do what Scripture says to do. Let's now look at a number of principles (with examples) that may inspire us to see the Church as the essential place to take our offerings—including our offerings of the talents God has given us.

Principle No. 1: Expect God to Use Your Talents Where You Least Expect It

Today Christian missionaries are working around the world to take the Gospel to those who have not heard. Sadly, this has not always been an emphasis in the Christian Church. When William Carey (1761–1834) was born, the Church at that time was extremely Calvinistic and completely uninterested in foreign missions. Therefore, when this young man found that he had an amazing gift for languages, he could see no way to use this talent in the Lord's work.

Carey became the pastor of a Baptist church, but as he read of the voyages of Captain Cook in the Pacific Ocean, God placed within him a desire to reach these peoples for Christ. To inspire those around him with this vision, he published the *Enquiry into the Obligations of Christians to Use Means for the Conversion of the Heathen*. He soon made plans to take his wife and four small children on the five-month voyage to India for the Gospel.

Carey began to realize that his gift for languages might be helpful in his ministry after all. He had learned Greek as a boy (in order to read the New Testament in the original language) and knew six other languages fluently. Now he learned Bengali so as to translate the Bible for those in India. By the end of William Carey's long ministry, he supervised the translation of the Bible into forty-four different languages, making the Word of God available for thousands of new converts.

Countless talents are needed for true ministry to go forth. I know a man who is a pipe fitter and wanted to serve the Lord with his talent. He became a mechanic with Mercy Ships, medically equipped ships that take surgeons (as well as the Gospel message) to many impoverished countries. My friend is talented neither in the operating room nor in the pulpit, yet his mechanical skills take doctors and ministers throughout the world.

Ask the director of any mission organization about the personnel needs; it might surprise you. They are often inundated with preachers, but desperately need pilots, mechanics, secretaries and cooks. Remember that the Bible says, "Whatever you do, work at it with all your heart, as working for the Lord" (Colossians 3:23). Using your talents will not only enable the Gospel to go forth in your own church but also encourage those around you to minister most effectively.

Principle No. 2: Give to Your Church, and Trust God to Give You Time to Enjoy Your Talents

Imagine being in charge of several thousand young nuns, plus having to teach, travel, write and consult with many people who look to you for wisdom and expertise. This was the life of Hildegarde of Bingen (1098–1179), a most fascinating personality of the Middle Ages.

This woman of God was surely one of the busiest persons alive in the twelfth century. She had given herself entirely to God's work and was sought for counsel by the church of her day. An authority in such diverse fields as medicine, theology, politics, art and natural history, she wrote brilliantly about each of these subjects and more. Hildegarde also possessed tremendous artistic talent; she was a gifted composer and playwright. She traveled extensively, making arduous overland missionary trips even into her eighties.

Where could she possibly find the time for such activities?

Since newspaper reporters were not around in the Middle Ages to interview this remarkable woman, we cannot know in detail how she would answer this question. But we do know that she found the time, somehow. Today, long after her administrative work is forgotten, her words and music live on. The many CDs of her beautiful music testify to the time she made for artistic endeavor.

You may think sometimes that you have no time to give to your church. Yet God seems to pay back double and triple to those who spend themselves on ministry to His children.

Let's never forget the words of Jesus: "Give, and it will be given to you" (Luke 6:38).

Principle No. 3: If Your Ministry Is Hindered, Seek Out a New Way to Minister

Christians can be enthusiastic starters, but our excitement often wanes when trouble blocks the path before us. We excuse ourselves, "Well, I guess God doesn't want me to do that after all," when a bit of persistence and tenacity could remove the roadblock—even though a course correction may be needed for final success. An American general once said, "When absolutely stymied, never decide to give up and go back; simply decide to find a different way to get there!"

Such a roadblock threatened to discontinue the ministry of John Bunyan (1628–1688): He was thrown into an English prison for twelve years. His crime was preaching without a license! As a lay preacher—"mending pots and pans by day and saving souls by nights and weekends"—he brought hundreds to the Savior. But the new king, Charles II, revoked the religious freedom of the previous reign, and Bunyan's tremendous talent for preaching was silenced by force.

Sitting in a dark jail with little hope of release, John Bunyan surely must have doubted if he would ever preach again. His family was impoverished, reduced to selling shoelaces to keep food on their table. How he must have wrestled with God! Was there no way to help his family and spread the Gospel? Surely he recalled the encouragement of Scripture: "Therefore, my dear brothers, stand firm. Let nothing move you. Always give yourselves fully to the work of the Lord, because you know that your labor in the Lord is not in vain" (1 Corinthians 15:58). Bunyan's answer was finally revealed as he discovered his talent for writing.

Instead of pining away during his long imprisonment, Bunyan began to work. Resourcefully, he wrote on the brown paper that wrapped the jugs of milk his wife brought to his cell. In his lifetime, John Bunyan authored fifty books, including the masterpiece *Pilgrim's Progress*. Finally published ninety years after his death, this book sold more than one hundred thousand copies in its first year and continues to be a bestseller. Bunyan's newfound talent for writing has furthered the Gospel for three centuries.

Principle No. 4: Use Your Home to Bless Those in the Church

The worldwide ministry known as the Navigators was founded in the 1930s by Dawson and Lila Trotman. When they married they had very little in the way of finances, but both had an intense desire to use their lives for Christ. Dawson's talent for motivating young men to live the Christian life led him to work with sailors on the California coast. Lila possessed a gift for hospitality that deeply touched the hearts of those to whom her husband preached.

Every evening, Dawson would bring sailors to their home for late-night discussions centered on God's Word. Lila welcomed each one and set out simple food for as many as twenty men without prior notice. Often the informal company stayed all night, the floor covered with sleeping sailors. This continued regularly for years, while the Trotmans raised five children of their own.

Lila and Dawson took Isaiah 60:11 personally as a verse that applied to their home: "Your gates will always stand open, they will never be shut, day or night." Their hospitality had a profound impact on young men who were often away from their homes for the first time in their lives. While Dawson challenged them in their Christian walk, these sailors looked to Lila as a second mom and were awestruck at the loving way she always opened her home to them.

Not everyone has this special gift—to be able to run a household filled nightly with hungry sailors. But each of us can improve in the area of extending hospitality to others. And if this is a talent you possess, use it all you can to the glory of the Lord!

Principle No. 5: Work for the Church with Fortitude and Diligence

Which scenario would you rather be in: someone late for work or someone late for church? You may answer, "Well, my pastor will forgive me, but my boss will not." As we have noted, this "I will be forgiven" attitude has created far too much complacency within churches today. When you are asked to do something for the church, do you invest the same amount of time and purpose you would for an important project at your job? Consider the example set by the great musician Johann Sebastian Bach (1685–1750).

The musical genius of J. S. Bach stands as a marvel through more than two and a half centuries after his death. When asked the secret of his genius, he answered simply, "I was made to work; if you are equally industrious you will be equally successful." It is doubtful that anyone has matched Bach's industriousness. His multitudinous scores took the Bach Gesellschaft forty-six years to collect and publish, and the completed edition filled sixty huge volumes.

Bach composed almost all of his music while fulfilling dozens of other tasks—working as an organist, a conductor, a music director, a private instructor, even a teacher of Latin to young boys, not to mention raising a large family and moving from post to post. The inspiration and beauty of his music are abundantly apparent. Yet the real mystery of Bach's life as a composer concerns *how* he found the time to write it all and polish it to perfection, not to mention how he created so many masterpieces cherished throughout the ages. Actually it is not such a mystery. Bach personified the Germanic Protestant work ethic. He truly lived the Scripture that says, "All hard work brings a profit, but mere talk leads only to poverty" (Proverbs 14:23). *I was made to work* could have been Bach's life motto.

This composer produced hundreds of masterpieces, such as his cantatas—written at the hectic pace of one per week. Knowing the time pressure, plus the fact that the composition would probably not be performed again for years (if at all), many composers would simply have filled the required pages with minimal effort. But Bach treated each work with the care of a master on his most renowned showpiece, knowing that he was preparing a work for a greater Master. He knew that God had "given him a trust" in his great musical talent, and he was determined to be faithful.

There are many times in our lives when a minimum effort will be noticed by no one and a maximum effort will be appreciated by no one. It is in those very times that we should realize who will acknowledge our greatest efforts. Often, the difference between a great work and a mediocre one is more than the genius involved; it is the care and extra work that perfect the final result.

Principle No. 6: Using Your Talents for the Church Does Not Decrease with Age

The world tries to tell us that using one's talents is for the young. In fact, we are made to feel less useful every year and told that aging must be avoided at all costs. Millions of dollars are spent every year on creams, facelifts and hairstyles that supposedly make us look younger. Yet as we age, we are maturing and receiving more experience that can be used for Christ.

An excellent example of someone who ignored the world's advice on this subject is Helena (c. 250–c. 330), mother of the Roman emperor Constantine. When her son became the head of the great empire, it was expected that Helena would settle for a life of luxury in palaces. Instead, she spent her "declining years" in ceaseless activity for the Christian Church.

In her late seventies, she traveled throughout the Holy Land, encouraging the faith. Her talents enabled her to master an enormous amount of details and technicalities: Helena sought out the original locations associated with Jesus' life and oversaw personally the construction of churches built at those sights in Jerusalem,

Bethany, the Mount of Olives and Bethlehem. Helena became a living example of the Scripture that says, "Even to your old age and gray hairs I am he, I am he who will sustain you. I have made you and I will carry you; I will sustain you and I will rescue you" (Isaiah 46:4).

If you are approaching your so-called "declining years," ask yourself: *Is God putting me out to pasture? Or is He calling me to use my talents for His Church?* Remember, for instance, that there are a great many young people who need encouragement, who need examples to follow. The second chapter of Titus exhorts the older members of the Body to train those who are younger. Never stop seeking ways to use your talents for Christ.

Principle No. 7: Always Give Your Very Best to Your Church

In the early 1500s the Christian Church was in upheaval. Excess and corruption in Rome had led to the Protestant Reformation, and throughout Europe was warfare and confusion. While powerful leaders fought over a multitude of issues, the common man tried to find where to fit in. Through it all, many on both sides attempted to use their talents for the Lord.

One of the greatest talents of that period (or any other!) was an Italian sculptor known as Michelangelo Buonarroti (1475–1564). He spent his youth learning and working in Florence, but soon moved to Rome and began to work for the Catholic Church. His first masterpiece, the *Pietà*, movingly depicted Mary holding Christ after He had been taken from the cross.

Later Michelangelo was asked to paint the ceiling of the Pope's private chapel, called the Sistine. It was a massive job, ten thousand square feet to be filled with pictures, all in fresco. The colors had to be ground with water, not oil, then quickly painted onto wet plaster. Michelangelo worked on his back, high on rickety scaffolding, for four long years. The result is a stupendous rendering taken from Genesis, the Creation to the Flood. Centuries later thousands line up every day to see the 343 figures of genius on the ceiling of the Sistine Chapel.

Michelangelo created many other masterpieces for his Church, from a huge sculpting of Moses to a seven-year painting of the Last Judgment. Yet he saved perhaps his greatest feat for his last. In his seventies Michelangelo turned architect and was appointed to complete St. Peter's Church. Its massive, double-shelled dome was the largest ever built, and Michelangelo lived to see its completion. It was as though he based his life on the inspiration of 1 Corinthians 9:24: "Do you not know that in a race all the runners run, but only one gets the prize? Run in such a way as to get the prize."

It was his determination to give God his very best that resulted in his Church's finest artistic treasures. The slightest detail, which others might have glossed over, was infinitely important to Michelangelo. He once stated, "Trifles make perfection, but perfection is no trifle." His genius, plus an overwhelming amount of work, has inspired millions through the last five centuries.

Principle No. 8: Use Your Talent for the Church in Quantity As Well As Quality

In chapter 5 we saw that, though we should never sacrifice quality for quantity, a good way to achieve higher quality is to increase our quantity. That is, the more we practice something, the better we become at it. This is true in everything from cooking to dancing, from business presentations to waterskiing.

It is also true in writing hymns. One of the most beloved hymn writers of all time was Francis Jane Crosby (1820–1915), better known as Fanny Crosby. When she was only six weeks old, she was permanently blinded by the incompetence of a doctor, yet her life was filled with joy and productivity. While attending a revival meeting, she was so moved by the Isaac Watts hymn "Alas! and Did My Saviour Bleed?" that she wholeheartedly gave her life to Christ.

Many of her beautiful hymns are still sung today, almost a century after her death. The list of favorites include "Safe in the Arms of Jesus"; "Nearer the Cross"; "All the Way My Saviour Leads Me"; "Jesus Is Tenderly Calling"; "My Saviour First of All"; "Rescue the Perishing"; "Tell Me the Story of Jesus"; "I Am Thine, O Lord"; "Take the World, But Give Me Jesus"; and her autobiographical classic, "Blessed Assurance."

Yet for every Fanny Crosby song that you can probably name, there are a hundred you have not heard. In her lifetime she wrote more than eight thousand hymns! For years she was under contract with a music publisher to submit three new hymns every week. Yet she was always careful to check and polish every one, never succumbing to sloppiness or mediocrity. In the midst of such industry, Crosby's zeal for Christ empowered her. She was a living example of Romans 12:11: "Never be lacking in zeal, but keep your spiritual fervor, serving the Lord."

Obviously, if one writes eight thousand hymns, it is quite unlikely that all of them will become classics. Perhaps many of them are not good at all. Yet Fanny Crosby knew that with each new hymn she was progressing in her skill. Every hymn writer would like to write such excellent compositions as the ten mentioned above. But those and many other favorites might have never been written if they were the only ones ever attempted by Fanny Crosby. Every classic like "Blessed Assurance" represents the behind-the-scenes work of a hundred others that were not as successful, yet each helped to create the true masterpieces.

Principle No. 9: Give to the Church Both in the Short-Term and in the Long-Term

The first half of the seventeenth century contained a plethora of literary geniuses, from William Shakespeare to John Donne. Into this atmosphere of talent came George Herbert (1593–1633), now considered one of the greatest Christian poets of all time. Yet most of his adult life was spent pastoring a small church in rural England.

This brilliant man finished college with many distinctions and entered public life with high promise. But after he had taught at Cambridge and served in Parliament, Herbert gave up all secular ambitions to devote himself to the Church. Rather than use his political connections to get a post of importance or comfort, he chose to pastor a country congregation in Bemerton near Salisbury. Herbert helped to rebuild the old church with his own funds and cared dearly for each member of his flock. He even penned a manual of practical advice to country parsons entitled *A Priest to the Temple*. This man of God was so loved and admired by those in his church that he was privately known throughout the countryside as "Holy Mr. Herbert."

This all took place in the 1630s, yet his ministry continues to this day. Why? Because in the midst of his "short-term" work to those around him in need, Herbert was constantly writing poetry that would make his name famous after his death. Indeed, on his deathbed Herbert sent many of his poems to be published only if they might do good to "any dejected poor soul." That same year some of his poetry was published with great acclaim and soon required thirteen printings to meet the demand.

This was Herbert's long-term ministry, which has helped and inspired millions whom he never met personally. As he embraced his local ministry, God exalted his writings to the highest circles—as the Word says: "Everyone who exalts himself will be humbled, and he who humbles himself will be exalted" (Luke 18:14). Much of Herbert's beautiful poetry is wildly creative and innovative, using visual as well as aural images, as in this excerpt from *Easter-wings:*

> Lord, who createdst man in wealth and store,
> Though foolishly he lost the same,
> Till he became
> Most poor:
> With thee
> O let me rise
> As larks, harmoniously,
> And sing this day thy victories:
> Then shall the fall further the flight in me.

There are many men and women who either find success in their own day and then fade away, or find no voice only to be recognized posthumously for their talents. George Herbert proves to us that one can do both. He found the critical balance between short-term ministry and a long-term legacy to those who would follow.

Principle No. 10: Use Your Talents to Discover and Encourage the Talents of Others in the Church

In the year 614 A.D. a girl was born in Britain who was to have a profound impact for Christ. Her name was Hilda (614–680), and she became the abbess of the monastery for men and women at Streanaeshalch (later renamed Whitby). Her reputation for brilliance and personal holiness spread throughout Europe; the Church's great Synod of Whitby in 664 was held at her monastery so that she might have a strong influence on the proceedings.

Many people assumed that Hilda's talent lay in organizing, as she kept her busy monastery in good order. But her primary gift was in recognizing and championing the talents of others. Of her many successes in this area, perhaps the greatest was that of discovering the talents of the poet Caedmon. The words of this godly artist, the first poet to use the English language in verse, have inspired thousands throughout the centuries. Yet Caedmon would probably have lived and died in obscurity if not for the notice and encouragement of Hilda.

The position of personnel manager is critical in every era. Anyone can recognize someone whose gifts have been nurtured and are in open use. But to see potential in someone takes a great talent indeed, just as only a trained eye can know a diamond in the rough. The Bible commands us to "encourage one another and build each other up" (1 Thessalonians 5:11). There are those among us who are called to be in the spotlight, and there are those of us whose job is to find the right person for that spotlight. Both are necessary talents.

Look about your church. Do you see talent just beneath the surface, awaiting someone's encouragement? Do you see potential that has yet to be honed and brought forth? Frankly, it takes talent to find talent. This may be your time to play the role of Hilda to your church's Caedmon.

Principle No. 11: Be Ready to Give Any Sacrifice to God's Work

God has a unique course for each of our lives, all within the covering of His Word. He calls some to cross the oceans in His service, while He directs others to minister right where they are. But each of us has this in common: We must cultivate a wholehearted desire always to accept His will for us, no matter what sacrifice is required.

In the late nineteenth century cricket was the sport of choice throughout Britain, as popular as football or baseball in contemporary America. The star player of that era was a young man named Charles Thomas Studd (1860–1931), known everywhere as "C. T." His athletic talents were outstanding and his exploits were cheered by thousands.

His father had come to Christ through a D. L. Moody revival, and a preacher visiting their home in 1878 led young C. T. to the Savior. But for six years he was more interested in cricket championships than the Lord's work: "Instead of going and telling others of the love of Christ, I was selfish and kept the knowledge to myself. The result was that gradually my love began to grow cold, and the love of the world began to come in. I spent six years in that unhappy, backslidden state."

Yet the Lord gave C. T. Studd another chance, bringing D. L. Moody directly into his life. The result was startling, and Studd now used every opportunity to witness for Christ. God gave this famous sportsman a heart for China where Hudson Taylor had begun missionary work. He later wrote: "It seemed as though I heard someone say these words over and over, 'Ask of me and I will give thee the heathen for thine inheritance, and the uttermost parts of the earth for thy possession.' I knew it was God's voice speaking to me, and that I had received my marching orders to go to China."

Opposition arose immediately. The Studd family was completely against this radical idea. His mother said that it would break her heart, even as her son wrote comforting letters: "Mother, dear, I do pray God to show you that it is such a privilege to give up a child to be used of God to saving poor sinners who have never even heard of the name of Jesus." The family started a campaign against his idea of mission work, even bringing in Christian workers to dissuade him from going.

The British public was equally aghast when Studd's plans were made known. Many pointed out what a shame it would be to have such a famous athlete, who could do such good for young Christians in England, to bury himself in the wilderness of China. Studd was unmoved: "I said, 'Let us ask God. I don't want to be pigheaded and go out there on my own accord. I just want to do God's will.'"

After months of prayer, Studd was still convinced of the Lord's leading. Despite the condemnation of many Christians and the tears of his family, he sailed for China in 1885 and spent the rest of his life in missionary work. Later this work took him and his family to live for years in both India and Africa. Studd found that as he had given his athletic talents back to God, the Lord gave him extraordinary preaching talents. The result was many thousands hearing the Gospel and giving their lives to Christ.

God may not call you to China, India or Africa—but if He does, are you ready to go? In 1906, when the penniless and frail C. T. Studd was turned down for missionary work in Africa by a committee of British businessmen, he replied, "Gentlemen, God has called me to go, and I will go. I will blaze the trail, though my grave may only become a stepping-stone that younger men may follow." He spent the next 21 years in Africa, bringing the Good News to peoples who would otherwise never have heard it. In 1931, after giving a long sermon, Studd went home to his Lord. The last word he spoke was *Hallelujah!*

Principle No. 12: Remember That Even the Quietest Acts of Service to Christ Serve as Examples to the Church

Public ministry is highly esteemed today. We applaud those who have visible displays of talent, who can thrive in the limelight. Those of us (the vast majority of Christians) who are called to be servants in the background may feel somewhat depressed as we consider what a small influence our little work may ever have. Yet God can use all of us for His glory. He used an obscure dishwasher of the mid-seventeenth century to show those around him how to worship the Lord continually—and he is still a great influence on our worship today.

Once Nicholas Herman (c. 1611–1691) entered a nearby monastery, he would henceforth be known as Brother Lawrence. He had no talents for leadership and was not a gifted speaker or teacher. His authorities— perhaps not knowing what else to do with him— assigned him to washing dishes. It was in the years of performing this mundane task that Brother Lawrence displayed his greatest gift.

His colleagues soon noticed that this simple man had an uncanny way of truly worshiping God in everything he did. Most of the brothers worshiped during their various church services, but Brother Lawrence worshiped continually as he went about his commonplace chores. He called it "practicing the presence of God."

He once explained this practice to his friends: "I turn my little omelette in the pan for the love of God. When it is finished, if I have nothing to do, I prostrate myself on the ground and worship my God—who gave me the grace to make it—after which I am happier than a king. When I can do nothing else, it is enough to have picked up a straw for the love of God."

Even on his deathbed, when asked what was in his mind, he replied, "I am doing what I shall do through all eternity. I am blessing God, praising him, worshiping him, and loving him with all of my heart."

Happily for us, the example of this remarkable man was not lost on his fellow monks. They urged him to write down the principles on which he based his life. The fruit of this effort was his *Practices Essential to Acquire the Spiritual Life,* in which he defines the practice of the presence of God: "That is, to find joy in his divine company and to make it a habit of life, speaking humbly and conversing lovingly with him at all times—every moment, without rule or restriction." This little book has been used by God for three centuries to bring Christians closer to their Savior.

What are the gifts, however obscure, that you can bring to your church? Could you visit the sick, make a meal for a shut-in, clean a church bathroom? I knew a dear saint at my church who cleaned the piano keys every week. No one else knew it except God and myself, but the keys always sparkled when I arrived on Sunday morning. His act of servanthood has always been an inspiring example to me. The Bible promises us that "humility and the fear of the Lord bring wealth and honor and life" (Proverbs 22:4).

The use of your talents, however simple, for Christ can be a great encouragement to those around you—whether in your home, in the church or (as we shall now explore) in the workplace.

To Consider and Discuss

1. What skills do you possess that might benefit your church?

2. How would you rate yourself in the area of hospitality? Think of a way you might improve in this area.

3. How difficult would it be for you to leave everything if God called you to a foreign mission field?

4. How can you assimilate Brother Lawrence's concept of practicing the presence of God into your life?

nine

Using Your Talents in the World

Live such good lives among the pagans that, though they accuse you of doing wrong, they may see your good deeds and glorify God on the day he visits us.

1 Peter 2:12

The concert lights are dimmed, and the audience falls silent and expectant. A powerful spotlight appears and you walk out on stage to thunderous applause. As you perform, you can sense that the listeners are on the edges of their seats. Your finish is met by ovations, curtain calls and encores. Afterward people form a long line waiting for your autograph. The next morning you read the excellent reviews praising your remarkable talent.

Then the alarm rings and you blearily wake up from your dream.

Very, very few of us experience such acclaim as the opening paragraph describes. Perhaps this is just as well. It is all too common for such mega-stars to be neurotic, unhappy and socially unbalanced. The pressure to perform perfectly every time is much too great for most of us to endure. We would crack under the strain. The annals of Hollywood, to name just one field of talent, are littered with drugs, divorces and suicides.

Most of us present our talents to the world without the pressure of a brilliant spotlight. Nevertheless, different pressures do appear that were not apparent when we used our talents in the home or the church. In these two places there is (generally) a degree of patience and forgiveness that is not always found in the workplace. If you burn a meal at home or find yourself late for a church meeting, you will not be fired. But such misdemeanors on the job could mean losing your livelihood.

It is not just the expectation of money (that is, wages) that increases pressure when we use our talents in the world. Usually our self-esteem is tied up in our jobs. Those who tend to lose themselves in their work become deeply depressed if they are laid off or fired. And many of those who do not use their talents may become dissatisfied with their jobs and face midlife crises, often leaving their positions for completely new (and often bizarre) careers. Thousands of others continue in their jobs but are unhappy and unfulfilled because their true talents are never utilized.

We can be most grateful that God has given important principles in His Word that relate to sharing our talents in the workplace. One of the most important is simply to realize that the Lord already has a plan for our talents, as explained in Ephesians 2:10: "We are God's workmanship, created in Christ Jesus to do good works, which God prepared in advance for us to do." This chapter will continue our examination of biblical principles before we make our final conclusions.

Principle No. 1: Never Allow Defeat to Keep You from Using Your Talents

The name of Abraham Lincoln (1809–1865) is well known as one of America's most respected presidents, but few remember the long road he endured to reach his place in history. In fact, winning the presidency in 1860 was one of the few races he ever won. Before that, his life had primarily been one of failure. Yet he never let defeat suffocate his talents.

Growing up in rural poverty, Lincoln had to fend for himself to acquire an education. As a young man he announced his candidacy for the Illinois legislature, but lost the election. He tried business but failed again. After practicing law he was elected to the U.S. Senate in 1846, but two years later was voted out. He tried again to run for senator in 1855, but did not even receive his party's nomination. The following year he attempted to be vice president for the Republican Party, but it selected someone else. When he finally ran for president in 1860, his victory was due to a split in the other party. He was a minority president, elected by fewer votes than the combined number of votes cast for the other two candidates.

Then came the tragedy of the Civil War. At many times the outcome of this conflict was uncertain. For the first two years there were more military victories for the South than for the North. Ultimately only Lincoln's determination was responsible for holding the country together. Although he lived only a few days after Lee's surrender, Lincoln's final days proved the veracity of his maxim: "Defeat is only a postponement of victory."

How often Lincoln must have been tempted to quit! Without a track record of success, he must have despaired many times as he listened to his critics. Yet he plodded faithfully onward, following the encouragement of Scripture: "You need to persevere so that when you have done the will of God, you will receive what he has promised" (Hebrews 10:36). When you consider throwing in the towel, consider how our country might have fared without the talents and perseverance of Abraham Lincoln.

Principle No. 2: Rejuvenate Your Talent with Enthusiasm

Like the apostle Paul, Wolfgang Amadeus Mozart (1756–1791) had to learn "the secret of being content in any and every situation, whether well fed or hungry, whether living in plenty or in want" (Philippians 4:12). His would be an unusual life. Instead of rags to riches, he lived a riches to rags story.

Young Mozart began as a prodigy, quickly winning the acclaim of the world. By the time he was six years old he was touring Europe and performing before the delighted courts and nobility of Europe. By his death at the age of 35, he was barely staving off poverty. What happened? Many things, including some of Mozart's own mistakes, but primarily a fickle audience that became indifferent once the child prodigy, such a novelty, became a man.

Yet in the worst of times Mozart never succumbed to paralyzing depression. When the pressures of money mismanagement overpowered him, Mozart would tear headlong into a brilliant new composition. When he saw other composers winning the public and denouncing his works, he would begin anew, writing innovative works that eventually eclipsed his competitors' best efforts.

Mozart had the wonderful virtue of refusing to allow circumstances to affect his musical output. When he obtained a commission he quickly fulfilled the request. He often lived without such an incentive, but he continued to create masterpieces, such as his last great symphonies composed without commission or even the prospect of an upcoming performance.

When we feel our talents are not being appreciated, we can learn a lesson from Mozart. Rather than let outward circumstances dictate our inner feelings and affect our fruitfulness, we can determine in our hearts to say, "This is the day the LORD has made; let us rejoice and be glad in it" (Psalm 118:24). Emerson hit the mark when he asserted: "Nothing great was ever done without enthusiasm."

Principle No. 3: Use Your Talent Even When It Hurts

When we think of the superb track star Jesse Owens (1913–1980), we remember his feats at the 1936 Olympics in Germany. These games were hosted by Adolf Hitler, in which he wanted to demonstrate to the world the superiority of the Aryan race. The Nazi dictator's plans were thwarted by this talented black man from America, who won three gold medals before Hitler's own eyes.

A year before this triumph, at the "Big Ten" meet in Ann Arbor, Michigan, Owens showed the world what he was made of. He had fallen down a flight of stairs, and it was doubtful he could still compete. But Jesse Owens was like this man of Scripture: "Though a righteous man falls seven times, he rises again" (Proverbs 24:16).

Receiving medical treatment right up to the time of the Big Ten meet, Owens begged his coach to allow him to run in the hundred-yard dash. He had previously set the world record in this event, 9.4 seconds. He wanted to run in it again, regardless of his pain. The coach relented. Owens won the race, tying his world record. Fifteen minutes later he persuaded his coach to allow his participation in the broad jump. Owens soared 26 feet 8.25 inches, breaking the old world record by almost half a foot. Immediately afterward he ran in the 220-yard dash and set another world record of 20.3 seconds. Finally he disregarded his injuries for one more race and broke yet another world record in the 220-yard low hurdles.

All these records, a feat never seen in the history of track and field, were set within a span of 45 minutes! These remarkable accomplishments were achieved not only by an injured athlete but by one who refused to quit even when it hurt. No one would have blamed Owens if he had elected to sit out this track meet. But he decided to persevere, and by the end of that special day Jesse Owens certainly had no regrets.

How much of an excuse does it take us to say no to a possible opportunity? Success is measured not only by how much we can accomplish but also by how much we have to overcome in order to accomplish. Our talents are hidden under a basket unless we have the courage and drive to use them—regardless of circumstances that would try to restrain or defeat us.

Principle No. 4: Use Your Talents to Witness for Christ

The inestimable talents of opera singer Jerome Hines have already been mentioned in chapter 6. Another incident in his long career illustrates how the faithful and responsible use of our talents can open a door for effective Christian witness.

Hines was once hired to sing in a production of Debussy's opera *Pelleas et Mellisande*. After rehearsals began, he was shocked to find that the director had "modernized" the opera by adding a prolonged sexual scene. What should Hines do? He had signed a contract but wanted nothing to do with this ungodly production. After considerable prayer he asked if he could speak to the entire cast. Conquering his fears, he quietly explained that, though he did not want to make things difficult for the company, he as a Christian man could not take part in this production.

The cast, none of whom was known to be a believer, had high respect for Hines' integrity. He had a reputation for hard work, encouragement and modesty. To Hines' surprise, the director agreed to remove the objectionable scene. This incident was repeated many times within the opera world. Hines' courage, reinforced by the steadfast use of his talents, enabled him to stand boldly for his Christian convictions. Indeed, throughout his career he has led many colleagues to the Savior.

When those around us reject the Gospel message, we need to ask ourselves, *Are they really rejecting Christ or reacting to our poor reputation? Have we truly lived a life that attracts people to the Good News, or have we selfishly used our talents to further ourselves and our agenda?* Long before we open our mouths in witness, our lives have become our witness, for good or otherwise.

Let's resolve to use our gifts to bless others so that when we have opportunity to speak for Christ, the way will have been prepared for us. The Bible admonishes us: "Be wise in the way you act toward outsiders; make the most of every opportunity. Let your conversation be always full of grace, seasoned with salt, so that you may know how to answer everyone" (Colossians 4:5–6).

Principle No. 5: Using Your Talents Means Breaking from the Crowd

Few women in history have had the impact of Margaret Thatcher, born in 1925. She was the twentieth century's longest-serving prime minister of England, and the first woman ever to hold that high position. Yet the "Iron Lady," as she was affectionately called by her many admirers, discovered that to use her talents, she had to break away from the crowd.

She learned this principle at an early age from the wisdom given by her devoted father. One of his many sayings that impressed her was, "You don't follow the crowd, you make up your own mind." Even when she entered the crowd-pleasing, vote-getting world of politics, Thatcher held principles and convictions that could not be shaken. While other politicians conformed their ideology to the winds of public opinion, she boldly proclaimed, "I'm not a consensus politician. I am a conviction politician."

Her convictions helped her stand up to Communist Russia, win a war in the Falkland Islands against an aggressive Argentina and break the power of British trade unions that had destroyed the three previous governments. Her determination to privatize state-run businesses turned such previously unprofitable companies as British Airways and British Steel into model industries. In all these actions Thatcher courageously broke the mold and followed her convictions, even when attacked by those in her own party. She was much more interested in serving her people's best interests than in following the dictates of the crowd.

Romans 12:2 commands us, "Do not conform any longer to the pattern of this world, but be transformed by the renewing of your mind." The talents God has given you can be hindered unless you determine to resist the pull of the world. If we hold painstakingly to our God-given convictions, our talents are freed to do that for which they were created.

Principle No. 6: Using Our Talents on the Side Can Still Have an Impact on the World

In the world of classical music, it often takes decades before the genius of a composer is universally recognized. The lack of public praise can be discouraging, and many composers earn a living in other ways while writing their music "on the side." But this does not make them failures.

A marvelous example is that of Charles Ives (1874–1954). Ives was the first great American composer, yet he was virtually unknown as a musician in his lifetime. His days were spent as an insurance executive and he co-founded a successful company. But late at night he toiled over his innovative music for year after unacclaimed year, producing vast quantities of incredible chamber music, songs, symphonies and piano repertoires.

Due to the extraordinary complexities of Ives' works, it was years before they were performed and appreciated. But at last Ives' genius was acknowledged by the musical community. Thirty-five years after its completion, his *Third Symphony* was finally performed—and then awarded the prestigious Pulitzer Prize for music.

He was not interested in worldly ambitions. Ives gave away his Pulitzer Prize money, remarking, "Prizes are for boys—I'm grown up!" Staunchly believing that his music should be available to all, he refused to copyright it. Ives finally acquiesced, but with the stipulation that the earned profits be used to help publish the works of younger composers.

Some of us have talents that are expressed by working on the side. At times we may despair of our gifting
ever being noticed. In those times remember the quiet
example of Charles Ives, who never let a lack of praise
or recognition prevent him from writing some of the
twentieth century's greatest compositions. In his day he
was unknown; today he is honored as one of America's
foremost composers. The last part of Proverbs 29:23
explains the life of Charles Ives: "A man's pride brings
him low, but a man of lowly spirit gains honor."

Principle No. 7: Remember That Using Our Talents Well Is the Best Example for Others

When two Jamaican immigrants to Harlem had a son
on April 5, 1937, it seemed unlikely that this child would
some day be considered one of America's greatest soldiers. Yet this was the humble beginning of General
Colin Powell, the first black officer to be named chair-
man of the Joint Chiefs of Staff—our nation's most prestigious military position. His parents urged him to
"strive for a good education." After joining the Army
Reserve Officers' Training Corps (ROTC), he was graduated in 1958 with the highest awards and commissioned a second lieutenant in the United States Army.

Wounded in his first tour in South Vietnam, Powell
then studied at the Command and General Staff College at Fort Leavenworth, Kansas. He finished second
in a class of twelve hundred. In Vietnam for a second
time, he received the Soldier's Medal for pulling a number of men from a burning helicopter. Powell's talent
for earning respect became so evident that in 1973 he
was assigned to command a battalion that was torn
with racial hostilities. His solution? "I threw the bums
out of the army and put the drug users in jail. The rest,

we ran four miles every morning, and by night they were too tired to get into trouble." His prescription worked perfectly.

In 1987 Powell was made National Security Advisor for the Reagan administration. A few years later he became known in every American household during the Gulf War, where he again demonstrated brilliant leadership and was awarded a congressional Gold Medal. As a colleague remarked about the general, "No one ever thinks of Colin as being black; they think of him as being good."

General Powell is cognizant of the example his life is to millions of young people, especially to African-American youth. He once told a reporter from *Ebony* magazine, "I've made myself very accessible to the Black press, and I do that as a way of just showing people, 'Hey, look at that dude. He came out of the South Bronx. If he got out, why can't I?'" Colin Powell is more than simply a gifted general; he is the modern embodiment of a person who can climb from the bottom to the top—a model for others to follow.

No matter who we are, someone is influenced by our lives. In that respect we are *all* leaders. Hebrews 13:7 tells those who follow the example of others to "consider the outcome of their way of life and imitate their faith." If we use our talents well, others will follow our example.

Principle No. 8: Find a Way to Serve Others

It may surprise you to consider a famous rock star—the Beatles' Ringo Starr, born in 1940—as an example of servanthood. But he was not always world famous. When Ringo first joined the group, replacing Pete Best as drummer, he endured humiliation that he has never forgotten.

The other three Beatles scheduled their first recording session for September 11, 1962. Unfortunately they forgot to tell their manager, George Martin, about the new drummer. When the excited young Ringo arrived at the studio, Martin told him to go home. A studio drummer had already been hired for the recording.

Instead of arguing, Ringo humbled himself and asked if there was anything he could do to help. If you listen carefully to the Beatles' first single *(Love Me Do* and *P.S. I Love You)*, you may notice marimbas and a tambourine far in the background. That rather insignificant role was played by Ringo. But his attitude of service was noticed and appreciated. There would never be another Beatles' song without Ringo on drums.

Our world tells us that the way up is to claw your way to the top. Our Lord tells us that the way up is to serve others with whatever talents you have: "For whoever exalts himself will be humbled, and whoever humbles himself will be exalted" (Matthew 23:12). The best way to use your gifts in this world is to find a way *to serve.*

Principle No. 9: Combine Your Talent with Thought and Prayer to Get the Best Results

Isaac Newton (1642–1727) was born on Christmas Day. He was so frail that the midwives thought that he would not survive. This genius lived 84 years and gave us far greater understanding of God's creation. Unlike many scientists, who work in groups to discuss news ideas among themselves, Newton worked best in isolation.

He insisted, "I had no special sagacity—only the power of patient thought." After graduation from Cambridge at the age of 23, he returned to his home in

Woolthrope "to meditate." Within eighteen months Newton worked out the laws of motion and universal gravitation, discovered the laws of the tides, proved with prisms that light is composed of all the colors of the spectrum, invented an improved telescope and developed a new mathematical system: calculus.

Such "meditation" proved useful indeed. When asked, "How did you discover the law of gravity?" Newton replied, "By thinking about it all the time." He would often sit motionless for hours, then suddenly run to a desk and write pages and pages without bothering to sit down. He truly believed that "it is the glory of God to conceal a matter; to search out a matter is the glory of kings" (Proverbs 25:2). Newton explained that his discoveries were made "by keeping a subject constantly before me until the first dawnings open little by little into the full light."

Fortunately for posterity, astronomer Edmund Halley saw the dozens of unpublished papers scattered on Newton's desk and offered to publish them at his own expense. The result was the *Principia,* perhaps the most important scientific book ever written. Newton's work on gravitational attraction demonstrates how to determine the mass of the planets and the sun, how to calculate the orbits of comets, and how the moon and sun pull the tides of the earth's oceans. Newton knew that such consistency could be explained only by the supreme genius of our Creator.

Isaac Newton humbly saw his place in God's world and never claimed the great praises heaped on him by his colleagues. Toward the end of his long and productive life, he wrote: "I do not know what I may appear to the world, but to myself I seem to have been only like a boy playing on the seashore, diverting myself in now and then finding a smoother pebble or a prettier shell

than ordinary, while the great ocean of truth lay all discovered before me."

Principle No. 10: Find the Good to Praise

Pablo Casals (1876–1973)—one the greatest cellists
of all time—inspired many students to follow in his foot-
steps. One was Gregor Piatigorsky. When he was first
given a chance to play for Casals, the young Piatigorsky
turned into a bundle of nerves. He played several pieces
horribly, yet was amazed to hear the great Casals praise
him again and again.

Years later, when Piatigorsky was himself a world-
class performer and a good friend of Casals, he mus-
tered the courage one night to ask about the undeserved
praise from that audition long ago. Casals remembered
that day instantly and grabbed his cello to play the very
sonata Piatigorsky had botched. "Listen! Didn't you play
this fingering? It was novel . . . it was good. And here . . .
didn't you attack that passage with an up-bow, like this?"
He continued for some time, finding good points about
Piatigorsky's performance. He concluded with the
words, "And for the rest, leave it to the ignorant and stupid who judge by counting only the faults. I can be grateful, and so must you be, for even one note, one wonderful phrase."

What an uncritical, encouraging attitude! It reminds
us of Paul's similar attitude as seen in the first chapter
of Philippians. In the fifteenth verse he referred to certain Christians who "preach Christ out of envy and
rivalry." Two verses later he pointed out that they
"preach Christ out of selfish ambition, not sincerely, sup-
posing that they can stir up trouble for me while I am
in chains." But the apostle, always looking for the good
he could affirm, concluded, "But what does it matter?

The important thing is that in every way, whether from false motives or true, Christ is preached. And because of this I rejoice" (verse 18).

This world has enough critics; it does not need us to join their ranks. Frankly it is easy to spot the mistakes of others. But if we can focus on the good that can be praised, God will use us and our talents to bless many people.

Principle No. 11: When You Know You Are Right, Do Not Let Anything Stop You

It is sometimes believed that successful people are those who do not have obstacles in their way. The truth is that successful people are those who overcome the obstacles in their way. To do this takes faith, perseverance and a determined belief that your cause is true. An excellent example of this principle is "El Libertador," the nickname given to Simón Bolívar (1783–1830).

The Spanish claim to South America had existed for two centuries when Bolívar was born in Caracas. Yet even as a young man, he had an inner conviction that his people should be free to govern themselves. When he was only fifteen years old, he argued this point confidently before the Spanish viceroy in Mexico City—to the latter's astonishment and alarm.

As a young man visiting Europe, Bolívar witnessed the coronation of Napoleon, which deeply grieved his heart. He had believed Napoleon to be a liberator of the people; now he saw that a new dictator had arisen. Later, while Bolívar was traveling in Italy, he made a vow to God on top of Mount Aventin that he would never rest until his people in South America were free. It would become a lifetime struggle.

Bolívar had many talents, especially as a military leader. But his major talent was communication: He had a tremendous ability to inspire the common man. Returning to Venezuela in 1807, he and his comrades began the struggle against Spain for independence. There were major setbacks, terrible military defeats and twice Bolívar had to flee for his life to other countries. But he always came back. He knew his cause was right.

On August 7, 1819, he and his army of revolution won a major victory in the battle of Boyaca. Other victories soon followed, and by the end of 1824 the last remnant of the Spanish armies was finally driven from the New World. Bolívar had only a few years to savor his triumphs, but his unswerving belief in the cause of liberty enabled him to become the "George Washington of South America."

Not many of us have such a huge responsibility as Bolívar, yet we all have important tasks God has given us to do—and certain talents with which to do them. A crucial Scripture for us is Galatians 6:9: "Let us not become weary in doing good, for at the proper time we will reap a harvest if we do not give up." We do not usually know when this harvest time will finally come, but if we stick to our purposes, we can be assured of God's promise of blessing.

Principle No. 12: Keep Using Your Talents Even Throughout a "Course Correction"

Millions of music lovers attend performances of *Messiah* every year. This magnificent piece, with its sublime "Hallelujah Chorus," was the result of a course correction in the life of a composer who refused to be defeated. George Frederic Handel (1685–1759) was born in Saxony but wrote his best works while living in England. He had written a number of successful operas and assumed that such compositions would be his life's work. But God had other plans for him.

Midway through Handel's career, the fickle public decided it was tired of operas. Although Handel toiled furiously, composing one opera after another, nothing seemed to work. The audiences deserted him, calamities ensued and financial disaster was imminent. The composer's health failed, and he surely must have wondered why God had abandoned him to such a hopeless position.

Handel's music career was not over, however, only his opera career. In hindsight we can see that God was arranging things so that Handel would compose in a new form, the oratorio. Taking stories from the Bible such as *Esther, Saul* and *Israel in Egypt,* Handel began to create one magnificent piece after another—and the audiences began to respond. It was in this new medium that he wrote his best music, including the classic *Messiah.* Thanks to this complete change of direction, his health, popularity and fortune returned in greater measure than he had ever known.

When we find ourselves unable to use our talents, it is difficult to have any hope for the future. But God has promised never to abandon us. He often uses circumstances to get our attention for a new direction in our lives. Instead of fighting God's will and clinging to what worked before, we need to seek the Lord for His divine guidance. His words assure us: "Whether you turn to the right or to the left, your ears will hear a voice behind you, saying, 'This is the way; walk in it'" (Isaiah 30:21). Perhaps God has an entirely unique course for us, in which He can greatly use our talents for His glory.

To Consider and Discuss

1. Lincoln's perseverance should prompt us to ask, How much does it take to make *me* give up?

2. On a scale of one to ten, how would you grade yourself in the area of enthusiasm?

3. How difficult is it for you to break away from the crowd in your talent area?

4. In what way is your life an example to those around you? How do you think you will be remembered by them?

Epilogue: Glorifying God and Changing Our World

"In the same way, let your light shine before men, that they may see your good deeds and praise your Father in heaven."

Matthew 5:16

We have looked at God's gifts of talent in many different ways. In the three parts of this book we have considered how your talents can be discovered, perfected and used for Christ. Among other ideas, we have examined the how, when and where of using these gifts. To conclude, we will ponder the why behind your gifting—that is, the question "Why did God give you talents?"

Ultimately there are three answers for this question, which may be represented by three words: *you, others* and *God.*

1. One of the reasons God gave you talent was simply to bless you. Considering the Lord's overwhelming love

for us, this should not be a surprise. He desires to "give good gifts" (Matthew 7:11) to His children and desires that we might be encouraged by using them. We often learn much about ourselves as we discover and use these gifts, and God uses them to give direction to our lives. Furthermore, some of us are able to use our talents for our livelihood and thus provide for our families. Yet even without such external rewards, we still find pleasure and happiness in the use of our talents, and this is as it should be.

Nevertheless, the *you* reason for our talents is surely the least important. It can be self-serving and produce narcissism, pride and conceit. We all know of talented but selfish people who use their gifts to bless them-selves—and no one else. This cannot be God's only desire for our talents.

2. We can also use our talents to bless others. We can inspire, comfort and encourage others by the unselfish use of our gifting. In this respect a pianist playing for a nursing home may be doing more good than a con-cert artist performing a concerto with a major orches-tra. Likewise a good executive provides needed jobs for his or her workers; an excellent teacher endows his or her students with quality education; a gifted painter gives the world another significant work of beauty and inspiration; and a skilled doctor may save our lives. Without question we are to use our talents for the bene-fit of others.

Yet it must be noted that such altruistic practices can be done with equal skill and consequence by unbeliev-ers as well as believers. Indeed, many of the most notable individuals, groups and organizations that use their tal-ents to bless others are, by their own admission, not Christian. This is still a wonderful thing to do, and we may all be glad that so many unbelievers are involved in benevolent activity. But a believer may fairly consider that there are specific ways in which he should use his gifts, based on his supernatural relationship with Jesus Christ.

3. Yes, as Christians we use our talents, first of all, for the Lord Himself. Most of us can easily agree with this statement in principle—but we are often left with a question: Exactly how do we use our talents for Christ?

The twofold response to this query is found in the title of this epilogue: Glorifying God and changing our world.

Glorifying God with Our Talents

On the night before the crucifixion, Jesus prayed to the Father: "I have brought you glory on earth by completing the work you gave me to do" (John 17:4). This tells us that in some mystical and wonderful way we bring glory to God when we do the work He has given us to do, including the proper use of the talents He has given us. We cannot see this with our natural eyes, yet it is an important article of our faith. For without it, much of the use of our talents can erroneously seem meaningless and barren to us.

Taking the words of Jesus quoted above, we see that a believing figure skater can glorify God while practicing diligently on the ice all alone—not just in a competition. We see that God can be glorified by the cook working in the kitchen, the student poring over textbooks, the accountant carefully balancing the myriad of figures and the mother telling her children stories with care and animation.

Notice the use of the word *can* in the above sentences. Being a Christian does not guarantee that everything we do automatically glorifies the Lord. We are not perfect yet! Even Paul admits: "Not that I have already obtained all this, or have already been made perfect . . ." (Philippians 3:12). Coming to Christ opens up *the opportunity* to use our talents to glorify God, but our attitude and intent are still critical factors.

Ultimately this is a matter of the heart, seen only by God Himself and utterly unable to be measured by man. If our hearts are filled with selfishness and pride, all our efforts will fall short of glorifying the Lord. But if our hearts are dedicated to giving our best for God, we may be assured that He is glorified indeed, whether or not our efforts are noticed by the world.

Changing Our World with Our Talents

There is even more that may be done for the Lord with our gifts. Anyone who has read the New Testament can see that God is interested in changing our world, bringing people out of darkness into His glorious light, saving the human race one by one. Our Lord's final instructions invite us to take part in this extraordinary work of proclaiming the Good News: "Therefore go and make disciples of all nations, baptizing them in the name of the Father and of the Son and of the Holy Spirit, and teaching them to obey everything I have commanded you" (Matthew 28:19–20).

Most of us are not full-time ministers, and we assume all too often that such verses are limited to the overt preaching of the Gospel. Yet even though we may not all be preachers, we have seen throughout this book that we *all* have been given talents. Is it possible, therefore, that using our gifting in a certain way can actually further this evangelistic work commanded by God?

In the Sermon on the Mount Jesus taught us to "let your light shine before men, that they may see your good deeds and praise your Father in heaven" (Matthew 5:16). The words *good deeds* can encompass more than the typical Boy Scout usage we usually attach to them. As we use our talents (that is, let our lights shine), we can join in the work God is doing to bring souls to Himself.

This assumes, of course, that the way we use our talents is indeed a good example to others, one that would inspire others to "praise our Father in heaven." Obviously if you are a mechanic working on someone's car and do a sloppy, incompetent job, your Father will not receive praise from the car's owner. (Neither will you; nor should you.) But if we take the time to use our talents with excellence and skill, then we are truly letting our lights shine, and these efforts can be a powerful witness to those around us.

The Little Drummer Boy

In this book we have examined many examples of using talents at home, in the church and in the workplace. Some will be more applicable to your life than others, but all display principles that can help you use your gifts with the greatest effectiveness. But if I had to give one illustration that best exemplifies the right attitude for using our talents, I would choose a character from a song we sing each Christmas season: the little drummer boy.

You remember the song—how a poor boy presents himself to the Christ Child and wants to give something to show his devotion. He decides to play his drum for the Babe. The words, told in the first person, relate the simple message:

> I played my drum for him,
> I played my best for him.

There is nothing more to be said. If, at the end of our lives, we can have a similar testimony—that we took our

God-given talents and "played our best for Him"—it will be enough. Then we, like our Lord Himself, will truly be able to say to the Father, "I have brought You glory by completing the work You gave me to do."

May God give each of us the grace one day to be able to say this to Him.

Dr. Patrick Kavanaugh is the author of seven books: *Worship—A Way of Life* (Chosen), *The Spiritual Lives of the Great Composers* (Zondervan), *Raising Musical Kids* (Vine), *Music of the Great Composers* (Zondervan), *Spiritual Moments with the Great Composers* (Zondervan), *The Music of Angels: A Listener's Guide to Sacred Music, from Chant to Christian Rock* (Loyola) and *Devotions from the World of Music* (Cook). As a composer he currently has eighteen compositions published by Carl Fischer, Inc., and is licensed by Broadcast Music, Inc. (BMI). Patrick has composed in a wide variety of genre, from orchestral to chamber music, from opera to electronic music. Reviews or articles concerning his original works and premieres have appeared in many national magazines, including *Music Journal, Christianity Today* and *Charisma,* and in major newspapers such as *The Washington Post, The New York Times* and *The Washington Times.*

He has served as director of the Washington branch of the National Association of Composers, as the classical music reviewer for *Audio* magazine in New York City and as minister of music at the Christian Assembly Center and the King's Chapel. For three years he was appointed to music panels of the National Endowment for the Arts. Patrick has lectured extensively at many universities and churches and at the National Portrait Gallery and the U.S. Department of State, and has appeared on many music and talk shows of both radio and TV.

Dr. Kavanaugh's education includes a Doctor of Musical Arts and a Master of Music from the University of Maryland, where he was awarded a full graduate fellowship for three years, and a Bachelor of Music from the CUA School of Music. He has also done extensive post-doctoral work in musicology, music theory and conducting. His teachers have included Earle Brown, Conrad Bernier, Mark Wilson and Lloyd Geisler. At the university level he has taught composition, music theory, music history and literature, counterpoint, orchestration and electronic music.

In addition to conducting many premieres of his own works, Kavanaugh was the conductor of the UM Twentieth Century Ensemble and the CUA Summer Orchestra. He now conducts regularly with the Asaph Ensemble. He also appears regularly as a conductor at the Kennedy Center Concert Hall and Terrace Theatre, Constitution Hall, the Center for the Arts, the Lisner Auditorium, the Alden Theatre, the National Presbyterian Center, Tawes Auditorium, the Folger Theatre and Gaston Hall. In 1993 he became the first American conductor to conduct an opera at Moscow's Bolshoi Theatre.

Patrick now serves full time as executive director of the Christian Performing Artists' Fellowship and is also the artistic director of the MasterWorks Festival in Winona Lake, Indiana. He resides near Washington, D.C., with his wife, Barbara, a cellist, and their four sons.

To contact Dr. Kavanaugh:

The Christian Performing Artists' Fellowship
P.O. Box 800
Haymarket, VA 20168
Phone: (703) 753-0334
Fax: (703) 753-0336
e-mail: CPAF@erols.com